GW01220864

WULFSTAN'S
CANONS OF EDGAR

EARLY ENGLISH TEXT SOCIETY

No. 266

1972

         ꝼ hæbbe·
hegoðe ⁊ huru pi hæ becc
 mæꞃꞃiᵹe þ he næbbe

 huꞃleꞅ ne abiꞃiᵹe

 ꞇonne mæꞃꞃiᵹe·

ꞃl þa þe heapꞅꞃy· ⁊ þ
ᵹe þ hiꞇ naꞃoꞃ ealdiᵹe·
man bꞃucan ne mæᵹe·
nū piꞅꞃe· ⁊ þa axꞃan
ᵹo ᵹꞇoꞃne ꞃeþe hiꞇ ꞃoꞃꞁi de·
ꞃꞇ leꞇe· þ he mæꞃꞃiᵹe·
biꞃiᵹe· þ iꞅ clæne oꞃ leꞇe·
þe mæꞃꞃian onᵹind·
þe þaꞃ ꞃul þinᵹ ꞇoðeð·
þa him ænᵹdon eꞇeð
on biꞃ meꞃ xꞃeᵹe budon·
ꞃꞃ· mæꞃꞃiᵹe· ⁊ ꞃ lꞅ þæꞇ
næꞃꞃe eꞅꞇ halᵹiᵹe·
o· þe man huꞃl on
man æniᵹ·
ꞃo de neah beon· ⁊ ꞇo
nlice ⁊ ꞃuꞃiðlice be hꞃoꞃ
ume· acᵹelo ᵹe man
e· ⁊ a ꞃy by ꞃnenðe leohꞇ·

WULFSTAN'S
CANONS OF EDGAR

EDITED BY

ROGER FOWLER

Published for
THE EARLY ENGLISH TEXT SOCIETY
by the
OXFORD UNIVERSITY PRESS
LONDON NEW YORK TORONTO

1972

© *Early English Text Society 1972*

PRINTED IN GREAT BRITAIN
AT THE UNIVERSITY PRESS, OXFORD
BY VIVIAN RIDLER
PRINTER TO THE UNIVERSITY

PREFACE

THIS is a parallel-text edition of an early eleventh-century set of ecclesiastical regulations, known generally as 'The Canons of Edgar'. It is in fact the work of Wulfstan, Archbishop of York, Bishop of Worcester, and chief statesman in the reigns of Ethelred and Cnut.

This edition differs from the previous ones of Thorpe and Jost in printing the whole text from Junius 121 as well as from Corpus Christi College, Cambridge, 201, and in offering a slightly longer text. Section I. 2 of the Introduction gives my reasons for regarding Junius 121 as a reliable text, and I hope justifies the printing of this text in full, instead of in footnotes as in Thorpe and Jost.

The edition was prepared originally as a thesis for the University of London degree of M.A. in English; this degree was gained in 1962, and the University gave permission for publication. My work on the thesis was well under way when Jost's edition of the *Canons of Edgar* (pp. 178–209 of *Die 'Institutes of Polity, Civil and Ecclesiastical', ein Werk Erzbischof Wulfstans von York*, Bern, 1959) came to my notice. The sources of the work which are quoted by Jost correspond closely to those quoted in my Commentary. I have acknowledged there the sources not found by me but quoted from Jost. As Jost's edition contains very little discussion of this important work, a full and independent edition has been thought desirable. Section I of the Introduction describes the text and the manuscripts in which it occurs, discusses the relationship between the D and X versions, and offers some new comments on the language of D. Previously scattered material on the authorship, date, and sources of the *Canons of Edgar* is collected in Sections II and III. Section IV attempts to argue the importance of the work in the canon of Wulfstan's known compositions, and discusses it in relation to Professor Bethurum's theory of Wulfstan's commonplace-book. The text, which gives glosses and alterations in footnotes, offers D and X on opposite pages, and is followed by some fragments occurring in MSS. Cambridge University Library, Add. 3206, and Brussels, Bibliothèque Royale, 8558–63 (2498). The comprehensive Commentary quotes sources and notes matters of interest.

PREFACE

I am most grateful to the Early English Text Society for agreeing to publish this work, especially to its Secretary, Mr. R. W. Burchfield, for constant guidance during the preparation for publication, and to his successor as Editorial Secretary, Dr. Pamela Gradon. My thanks go to many individuals who assisted me by giving advice and information, and by reading drafts, when the work was in preparation as a thesis and subsequently as a book: to my examiners, the late Professors A. H. Smith and G. N. Garmonsway; to Mrs. Margaret 'Espinasse; to J. Norton-Smith, for help with the glosses to X; and to Geoffrey Needham, for many hours of fruitful discussion in the earliest stages. Above all, I owe a special debt of gratitude to Professor Dorothy Whitelock, who gave help and advice unstintingly while the thesis was being revised for publication. Those of her suggestions which I have incorporated are too many to acknowledge separately, although her advice on the rewriting of Section I. 3 merits special mention.

R. F.

CONTENTS

Corpus Christi College, Cambridge, MS. 201, p. 99 *Frontispiece*
Bodleian MS. Junius 121, f. 28

PREFACE   v

ABBREVIATIONS   ix

INTRODUCTION

  I. *The Manuscripts*
    1. Description of the manuscripts   xi
    2. The versions of the *Canons of Edgar* in the three manuscripts   xvi
    3. The language of D and X   xx

  II. *Authorship and Date*   xxvi

  III. *Sources*   xxxiv

  IV. *The Relationship of the* Canons of Edgar *to Wulfstan's other Works*   xlv

NOTE ON THE TEXT   lxii

THE CANONS OF EDGAR   1

APPENDIX I. The text of *Canons of Edgar* 1, 2, 5–8 in Cambridge University Library MS. Add. 3206 (Cu)   20

APPENDIX II. The text of Brussels, Bibliothèque Royale MS. 8558–63 (2498), f. 140   21

COMMENTARY   22

BIBLIOGRAPHY   43

GLOSSARY   47

ABBREVIATIONS

MANUSCRIPTS

Bx   Brussels, Bibliothèque Royale, MS. 8558–63 (2498)
Cu   Cambridge University Library, MS. Add. 3206
D   Corpus Christi College, Cambridge, MS. 201
X   Bodleian, Oxford, MS. Junius 121

PRINTED BOOKS

Ælfric I (II, etc.)   Ælfric's *First OE. (Second OE.*, etc.) *Pastoral Letter*, ed. B. Fehr, *Die Hirtenbriefe Ælfrics in altenglischer und lateinischer Fassung, Bibliothek der angelsächsischen Prosa*, ix, Hamburg, 1914, reprinted, with a supplement to the Introduction by Peter Clemoes, Darmstadt, 1966.

Ancient Laws   B. Thorpe, *Ancient Laws and Institutes of England* (folio edition), London, 1840.

Benedictine Office   *The Benedictine Office*, ed. J. M. Ure, Edinburgh, 1957.

Bosworth–Toller   J. Bosworth and T. N. Toller, *An Anglo-Saxon Dictionary*, Oxford, 1882–98; Supplement, 1908–21.

E.E.T.S.   Early English Text Society.

E.H.R.   *English Historical Review.*

'Einige Wulfstantexte'   K. Jost, 'Einige Wulfstantexte und ihre Quellen', *Anglia*, lvi (1932), 265–315.

Gesetze   *Die Gesetze der Angelsächsen*, ed. F. Liebermann, Halle, 1898–1916.

Homilies   *The Homilies of Wulfstan*, ed. D. Bethurum, Oxford, 1957. References to the homilies use the numbering of Professor Bethurum's edition, except where explicitly given otherwise.

Ker, *Catalogue*   N. R. Ker, *A Catalogue of Manuscripts Containing Anglo-Saxon*, Oxford, 1957.

J.E.G.Ph.   *Journal of English and Germanic Philology.*

Napier   A. S. Napier, *Wulfstan: Sammlung der ihm zugeschriebenen Homilien nebst Untersuchungen über ihre Echtheit*, Berlin, 1883.

NPL   Northumbrian Priests' Law, *Gesetze* I, 380–3.

PL   *Patrologiae Latinae Cursus Completus*, ed. J.-P. Migne, Paris, 1864–81.

ABBREVIATIONS

P.M.L.A.   *Publications of the Modern Language Association of America.*

Polity   K. Jost, *Die 'Institutes of Polity, Civil and Ecclesiastical', ein Werk Erzbischof Wulfstans von York*, Bern, 1959.

Sermo Lupi   *Sermo Lupi ad Anglos* ed. D. Whitelock, 3rd edition, London, 1963.

T.R.H.S.   *Transactions of the Royal Historical Society.*

INTRODUCTION

I. THE MANUSCRIPTS

1. DESCRIPTION OF THE MANUSCRIPTS

D. *Corpus Christi College, Cambridge, MS. 201*[1]

THIS is an eleventh-century manuscript of about 280 × 162 mm. N. R. Ker divides it into two volumes: I, pp. 1–178; II, pp. 179–272.[2] II is an Exeter manuscript containing Theodulf's *Capitula* and an OE. translation of the *Capitula*; it is a companion volume to MSS. C.C.C.C. 191 and 196.[3] C. H. Turner divides I into two volumes, pp. 1–146 and 147–78, and Professor Bethurum follows this division.[4]

Ker detects four hands, and two main stages of composition, in I, the volume which concerns us;

A. (*a*) pp. 1–7, 161–7, the first leaves of two quires.
B. (*b*) pp. 8–151, 167–9.
   (*c*) pp. 151–60.
   (*d*) pp. 170–6 (pp. 177–8 are blank).

The *Canons of Edgar* is copied out by hand (*b*) on pp. 97–101. This is a clear round hand, occupying 41 ruled lines to each page. The heading is in small red capitals; section 1 begins with a large red capital of about 35 mm.; the initial A of other sections is alternately red and green, about 1 cm. There is some deliberate variation in the curvature or angle of the central bar, which appears as ⌵ or ⌴. The left upright is often decorated with various loops and curves. The period is used frequently, sometimes where a comma would be placed in modern punctuation, sometimes to mark off short phrases. Accents are used, very infrequently, to

---

[1] Described by M. R. James, *A Descriptive Catalogue of the Manuscripts in the Library of Corpus Christi College, Cambridge* (Cambridge, 1912), i. 485 f.; N. R. Ker, *A Catalogue of Manuscripts containing Anglo-Saxon* (Oxford, 1957), pp. 82–91; L. Whitbread, 'MS. C.C.C.C. 201: a Note on its Character and Provenance', *Philological Quarterly*, xxxviii (1959), 106–12.

[2] Ker, op. cit., nos. 49 and 50. Vol. I only (Ker 49) is henceforth referred to as D.   [3] Ibid., nos. 46 and 47.

[4] C. H. Turner, *Early Worcester Manuscripts* (Oxford, 1916), p. lvii; *Homilies*, p. 2. Ker's description of the manuscript was not available when *The Homilies of Wulfstan* was published.

show vowel length, as in *Canons* 16 *arǽre*. I have not shown these. A heavy curved accent ⌒ appears four times in *Canons* 53, and is possibly an addition, as this section shows signs of modification. Alterations are few, and these are all shown in footnotes.

The date of D is not easy to fix. Professor Bethurum assigns it to the 'late eleventh century' with no comment.[1] In this she follows Schlemilch,[2] Feiler,[3] and Liebermann.[4] Professor Whitelock dates it nearer the middle of the century.[5] Ker also favours the middle of the century for that part of volume I which concerns us (pp. 8–160, 167–76).[6]

D is a major source of Wulfstan's homilies. It contains Ia, Ib, II, III, IV, V, VII, VIIa, VIIIa, VIIIc, IX (in part), Xb, Xc, XI, XIII, XVIb, XIX, XX, and XXI.[7] The other principal contents are the *Benedictine Office*; parts of *Polity*, Ælfric's *First OE. Letter for Wulfstan* (Ælfric II) rewritten in Wulfstan's style; the *Northumbrian Priests' Law*; and the following legal codes: I Athelstan, I Edmund, II and III Edgar, V, VI, VIIa, and VIII Ethelred, parts of I and II Cnut; the OE. translation of *Apollonius of Tyre*; five of the short legal codes which Professor Bethurum ascribed to Wulfstan.[8]

The contents of D associate it with Wulfstan and Worcester, especially as they correspond in general to the contents of two manuscripts (taken together) which are unquestionably of Worcester origin: Hatton 113 and Junius 121.[9] On the strength of this similarity Wanley attributed it to the Worcester scriptorium,[10] as did Turner; Feiler agreed with Liebermann's suggestion that the manuscript might have come from one of the dependent houses of Worcester.[11] In fact, there is no evidence, other than that of the contents, to connect it with Worcester. There is no palaeographical

---

[1] *Homilies*, p. 2.
[2] *Beiträge zur Sprache und Orthographie spätaltengl. Sprachdenkmäler der Übergangszeit, 1000–1150*, Studien zur englischen Philologie, xxxiv (1914), p. xiii.
[3] *Das Benediktiner-Offizium* (1901), p. 8.
[4] *Gesetze* I, xxii (1050–80).
[5] 'Wulfstan and the Laws of Cnut', *E.H.R.* lxiii (1948), 437; for a more recent description, see 'Wulfstan at York', in *Franciplegius*, pp. 221–2.
[6] Ker, *Catalogue*, pp. xvi, 82.
[7] The numbering of homilies is that of Professor Bethurum's edition unless otherwise indicated.
[8] D. Bethurum, 'Six Anonymous OE. Codes', *J.E.G.Ph.* xlix (1950), 449 f.
[9] On Hatton 113, see Ker, *Catalogue*, pp. 391–9; on Junius 121 (X) see below.
[10] G. Hickes, *Thesaurus* (1705), ii. 141.
[11] Feiler, op. cit., p. 8, n. 2; *Gesetze* I, xxii.

INTRODUCTION

evidence to connect it with any particular scriptorium; on the contrary, the script is quite unlike that of the 'Wulfgeat' manuscripts, and it may be thought significant that there are no glosses in the 'tremulous' Worcester hand.[1] Linguistic evidence points to a place of origin other than Worcester: see below, pp. xx ff.

The known history of the manuscript begins in the sixteenth century with Archbishop Parker. He perhaps acquired it from Edward Cradock, Lady Margaret Professor of Divinity at Oxford from 1575 to 1594. He gave it to Corpus Christi College, Cambridge: it appears in Thomas James's Corpus Catalogue of 1600.[2] It was rebound in the eighteenth century and again in 1948.

X. Bodleian MS. Junius 121[3]

This is again an eleventh-century manuscript, of 263 × 153 mm., containing vii+161 pp.

The *Canons of Edgar* occurs on ff. 25^v–31^v. There are 23 lines to each page. The work is written out as part of *Polity*, with the chapter number, XX, alongside the heading ITEM SINODALIA DECRETA. Section 1 starts with a red R of 21 mm., and the first line is in capitals larger than those of the heading. The work is not paragraphed, unlike the version in D, but each section is distinguished by its large initial ampersand, 8 mm. high, and raised, as against the 4-mm. 'lower-case' ampersand within the sections. F. 29^v has an ornamental Æ(-rest *Canons* 54); 30^r has a large S(-e canon *Canons* 65a); 30^v a decorative D(-unstan *Canons* 68c); 31^r a large G(-if man *Canons* 68 f). The *Canons* is heavily annotated and corrected by hands of all periods, and I have given in footnotes all the OE. and Latin glosses, additions, and corrections. There appear to be at least four separate hands annotating this part of X; I have identified these as 1–4. 1, providing the great majority of the glosses, is the 'tremulous' Worcester hand.[4] This shaky, backward-sloping hand, dated by Ker c. 1225–50,

---

[1] See N. R. Ker, 'The Date of the "Tremulous" Worcester hand', *Leeds Studies in English and Kindred Languages*, vi (1937).

[2] M. R. James, op. cit., p. 1 (50). On Parker's connection with D, see Ker, *Catalogue*, pp. 90 and lii–liv.

[3] Described in *A Summary Catalogue of Western Manuscripts in the Bodleian Library* (1937), II, part ii, pp. 989–90 (no. 5232); Ker, *Catalogue*, pp. 412–18 (no. 338); cf. J. M. Ure, *The Benedictine Office* (Edinburgh, 1957), pp. 3–9.

[4] N. R. Ker, *Leeds Studies in English*, vi (1937); S. J. Crawford, 'The Worcester Marks and Glosses of the Old English Manuscripts in the Bodleian', *Anglia*, lii (1928), 1–28.

glosses almost always in Latin. This hand varies in blackness, but is always characterized by uncertainty, imperfect joining of strokes, and a pronounced backward slope. 2 is a firmer hand, and occurs much less frequently. 3 is a large untidy hand with long ascenders and descenders which makes, for example, the addition *þa hwile þe his lif sig* to *Can.* 8. 4 is a small and very neat hand which makes OE. additions and corrections, e.g. those to *Can.* 18 and 20. 1 and 4 are the most frequent and important of the four hands.

Besides the *Canons of Edgar*, the principal contents of X are parts of *Polity*, the *Benedictine Office*, Homilies Ib, Xa, and XIX, several of Ælfric's homilies, Ælfric's *Pastoral Letters* I and III, and a selection of canonistic and penitential literature.

The manuscript is connected with Worcester by this inscription on f. 101[r]:

Me scripsit wulfgeatus scriptor wigornensis. ora obsecro pro ipsius neuis cosmi satorem. amen. Et qui me scripsit semper sit felix. AMEN.

N. R. Ker thinks this is copied from the exemplar of the manuscript,

since it begins on the same line as the end of the preceding text and comes at a point where there is not a decided break, nor a change in the appearance of the writing.[1]

Even though this manuscript was not copied by Wulfgeat, it was at least copied from a manuscript written by that Worcester scribe; it is written in a hand which appears in other Worcester manuscripts, e.g. Hatton 113 and C.C.C.C. 178; the dialect of the manuscript is entirely consistent with that of Worcester in the eleventh century; and the contents of the manuscript connect it with several known Worcester manuscripts.

X was still at Worcester in the late-twelfth/thirteenth century, for it contains glosses in the 'tremulous' Worcester hand, and also a copy of the Nicene Creed in the same hand on f. vii.[2] In 1622–3 it was still at Worcester, according to Patrick Young's catalogue; it may then have passed through the hands of Dugdale, Lord Hatton, and John Fell, later Bishop of Oxford, who gave it to the Bodleian in 1678.

Ker dates Junius 121 in the third quarter of the eleventh century, and this date would now be generally accepted.[3]

---

[1] Ker, *Catalogue*, p. 417.
[2] For a facsimile, see Crawford, op. cit., opposite p. 1.
[3] **Ker,** *Catalogue,* pp. xviii, 412. For a concise paragraph on the date, see p. 5.

Cu. *Cambridge, University Library Additional MS. 3206*[1]

A fragment of four pages, from the second half of the eleventh century, mutilated through being used as a pastedown for an octavo book. The text corresponds to that of ff. 22ᵛ/8–26ʳ/13 of X, and p. 4 (162 × 108 mm.) includes *Canons* 1–2, 5, 6, 7, and part of 8. X's heading is omitted by Cu, although the preceding material is the same as in X. Our text takes up lines 9–27 of p. 4. Line 9 begins with a red R of 8 mm.; the first three words are in small capitals. The handwriting is small and neat, 'rather pointed' as Ker says, and quite legible although the page is somewhat stained. The right-hand side of the page has been trimmed and about three letters are lost at the end of each line. The bottom of the page also has been trimmed, leaving only the tops of the letters of line 27, but enough is left for reconstruction by comparing with *Canons* X, 8. The full text is given in the Appendix.

Bx. *Brussels, Bibliothèque Royale, MS. 8558–63 (2498)*[2]

A manuscript of 153 leaves, divided by Ker into three parts: A, 1–79; B, 80–131; C, 132–53. A consists of the enlarged Rule of Chrodegang of Metz, with six OE. glosses of the tenth century. B has an imperfect copy of the *Penitential of Pseudo-Theodore*, the first six lines of which are glossed in OE. (again tenth century). C (132–9) contains a set of penitential texts, all but the first in OE., which occur in various forms in a number of manuscripts connected with Wulfstan.[3] 140ᵛ–53ᵛ contain various penitential pieces.[4] These two parts of C are in different eleventh-century hands. We are concerned with the contents of f. 140ʳ, which was originally left blank and filled in 'in a poor sloping hand of the earlier part of

---

[1] Described by Ker, *Catalogue*, p. 10 (no. 11).
[2] Described by Ker, *Catalogue*, pp. 8–10 (no. 10).
[3] They occur, more or less complete and in various orders, in Bx (Ker, no. 10), ff. 132–9; D (Ker, no. 49B), pp. 114–25; C.C.C.C. 265 (Ker, no. 53), pp. 72–83; Cotton Tiberius A. iii (Ker, no. 186), ff. 44, 55–6, 94ᵛ–6; Junius 121 (Ker, no. 338), ff. 65ᵛ–7ᵛ; Laud Misc. 482 (Ker, no. 343), ff. 28ᵛ, 40–6. According to Wanley, they once were extant in the now damaged Cotton Otho B. x (see Ker, no. 177B, pp. 227–8), ff. 160ᵛ–4ᵛ. Thorpe printed from D as part of the *Canons enacted under King Edgar*, and Mone (*Quellen und Forschungen*, 540–7) and Raith (*Die altenglische Version des Halitgar'schen Bussbuches*, 1933, p. 76) have both printed parts. See also Fowler, 'A Late Old English Handbook for the Use of a Confessor', *Anglia*, xxxiii (1965), 1–34, a complete edition from all the manuscripts.
[4] For details see Ker, *Catalogue*, p. 9, art. 2.

s. xii'.¹ This page, printed by Mone,² is re-edited as a second appendix to the present text. It contains sentences which parallel fairly closely *Canons* 2, 12, 13, and 68b, and *Northumbrian Priests' Law* 25.³

Ker describes the language as 'South-Eastern'. The following non-WS. forms occur: *wexe, forwerne, geændie, ænde, geberige, selfen, heren, eldren, nenne, scænde, geof, geberde, preste, berege*.

2. THE VERSIONS OF THE CANONS OF EDGAR IN THE THREE MANUSCRIPTS

A. *Cu is closer to X than to D*

Cu agrees with X in every case where X differs from D; e.g.:

Can. 1: X PREOSTAS, Cu preostas: D Godes þeowas.
        X, Cu on fultume and on helpe: D to fultume and helpe.
        X, Cu æfter Godes rihte: D omits.
Can. D3, D4: X, Cu omit.

The agreement between Cu and X in these cases may be due to dependence on a common exemplar, or to Cu's dependence on X or vice versa. It would be difficult to choose between these alternatives, as Cu is too slight for its date or place of origin to be determined.

B. *X and D represent two different versions at an earlier stage*

There are some major differences of wording which presuppose different original versions, as opposed to the addition or omission of words, phrases, or sections which can be put down to later interference with the text by scribal error or revision. The number of variants between D and X makes it difficult to believe that either D or X could be a copy of the other; nor could they be descended from a common model: the variants are too extensive to be explained as the errors of a single stage of copying from a single model. Many variants can be explained as scribal errors. Others, for example the omission from X of *Canons* 3, 4, and 70, may be a result of the revision of the text for inclusion in *Polity*. Some of

---

[1] Ker, loc. cit.
[2] F. J. Mone, *Quellen und Forschungen zur Geschichte der teutschen Literatur und Sprache* (1830), p. 547.
[3] *Gesetze* I, 381.

the additions in X, for example 68b–i, may date from the same revision: these particular sections are copied from VIII Atr. 28–30, 19–24, which is later than the *Canons*, and so they cannot have been in the original text.[1] But after such variants have been explained, there remain several which point to quite separate versions of the original, or at least of the exemplars of D and X. These are to be found in *Canons* 16, 39, 43, 46, 49, 50, and 54,[2] of which 16 and 46 may be examined here for illustration.

Canons 16. The presence of extra material in X (*and ðone deofles cræft . . . eorðan tihð* and *on geares niht*) may be explained as the result of a simple process of addition to X or omission from D. But the rewording of the proscription of the worship of trees and stones represents a more complex revision. In X *treowwurðunga* and *stanwurðunga* are just two of a list of similar nouns; in D a different phrase is used (*and eac on oðrum mistlicum treowum and on stanum*), which has been written afresh for its new context, and is so well integrated that it refers back to the preceding *ellenum*. This is not a mere scribal shift of material; it may be a relic which points to two alternative versions.

Canons 46. The insertion of *mynsterpreosta*[3] in D and *gewæpned* in X alters the sense of the two sentences. The passage in X contains two distinct ideas instead of one, and the rhetorical balance of clauses is different in the two sentences. In D the balance is between *mæssepreosta* and *mynsterpreosta*, and between *circan dyra* and *weohstealle*; in X there is a complete shift of emphasis, *gewæpned* being balanced against *cyrican dura*, and *weofodstealle* against *oferslope*.

Because of the extent of the difference between D and X, which suggests that they may go back to different versions of the original, I have given both texts in full, in parallel form for ease of comparison.

c. *X is in many respects superior to D*

Another reason for printing X in full is that it frequently gives better readings than D, and is altogether a more respectable text than has hitherto been supposed.[4]

---

[1] See discussion, Commentary under *Can.* 62.
[2] None of the lists of variants given in this section is meant to be exhaustive.
[3] See Commentary under *Can.* 46.
[4] Both Thorpe and Jost print extra material from X in footnotes only, even though some of it must be granted authenticity.

INTRODUCTION

At some point or points in its line of transmission X has been extensively modified, with the consequent loss of *Canons* 3, 4, 21, and 70,[1] re-positioning of 61 at 68a, and addition of 65a, 68b–i; perhaps at the time when the *Canons* was rewritten as part of *Polity*. The loss of these sections is unfortunate, but no detriment to the study of X as a text of the *Canons* in its own right: the state of the X text towards the end is by no means as puzzling as at first appears, as the additional material is obviously spurious (its departure from the formula *and riht is* is a clear enough indication that it is foreign), and the missing material is not extensive. A 'reconstruction' from both texts of *Canons* 56–70 is implied in my scheme of numbering.

The loss of four sections of X is compensated by the gain of three: 56, 66, and 67. These three sections are probably genuine, since they use sources habitual to the *Canons of Edgar*. They enable Thorpe's and Jost's 67 sections to be increased to 70. This gain should make one hesitate to dismiss X as inferior because it has obviously been modified: the modification is so obvious that it can easily be allowed for when an attempt at reconstruction is made. Not only is X valuable in helping to reconstruct the contents of the prototype; it also gives better readings than D in a number of places: readings more in accord with the sources, fuller readings, and readings which simply make better sense:

Canons 1. X æfter Godes riht: D omits.
    (Cf. Homily Xc, 166 hold 7 getrywe his worldhlaforde æfre mid rihte.)
   15. X fulluhtes and scriftes: D fulluhtes.
    (Cf. *NPL* 8 Gif preost fulluhtes oððe scriftes forwyrne.)
   15. X vii. nihtum: D xxx.vii. nihtum.
    ('Seven days' agrees with Ælfric 2, 163, and there is no parallel for thirty-seven, which in any case is hardly consistent with the urgency of baptism.)
   16. X and þone deofles cræft . . . tihð: D omits.
    (Cf. *Penitential of pseudo-Ecgbert* IV, 16.)
   20. X wæda: D ræda.
    (Cf. *Excerptiones pseudo-Ecgberti* CLIV, Ælfric I, 114–15; II, 206; 2, 175.)

[1] The fact that the source of 3 and 4, *Theodulf's Capitula* (ch. iv), is used extensively throughout the text makes it highly probable that these sections formed part of the original; a similar argument applies to 21 and 70. (See Commentary to these sections for the sources in question.)

29. X gecwemde: D gecweme.
    (Past tense makes better sense here.)
42. X fules: D omits.
50. X efenforðe: D efenweorðe.
54. X leohtgesceotu... : D omits.
    (Cf. Homily XIII, 77-8, V Atr. 11-11, 1, and later codes.)

Compared with this list of nine superior readings in X, there are only three better readings in D:

Canons 16. D arære: X lære.
       19. D folcgemota:[1] X omits.
       38. D forgimde: X forgyme.

Even more suggestive of the greater reliability of X are some of the corrections and glosses in this manuscript:[2]

Canons X8. hæbbe þa him to rihtæwe (þa hwile þe his lif sig).
            (Cf. Ælfric I, 73, þa hwile his dagas beoð.)
       X18. freolsdagum (æt cyrcan).
            (Cf. *Penitential of pseudo-Theodore* XXXVIII, 9: ad ipsas aecclesias.)
       X37. þriwa (crossed out and *twiga* written above).
            (Cf. Ælfric 3, 75.)
       X41. calic (gloss: Gylden oððe seolfren tinen).
            (Cf. Ælfric I, 58: Gylden oððe seolfern oþþe tinen.)

The last three of these corrections are in the same small, neat, eleventh-century hand. All bring the *Canons* nearer to its sources. The phrases from Ælfric I added to *Canons* 8 and 41 occur in X's version of Ælfric I. We can infer from these corrections that the scribe who made them was familiar with Wulfstan's sources for the *Canons*, and with the 'commonplace-book'.[3] X is one of the commonplace-book manuscripts, and the scribe who corrected the *Canons* in X could have found two of his corrections within the same manuscript. X definitely comes from Worcester; D perhaps does not. X is carefully corrected by scribes who had the use of Wulfstan's commonplace-book, and knew how he had used it. X gives a number of better readings than D, in some cases is nearer the sources, and in one case, that of *Canons* 54 *leohtgesceotu*, agrees with a work derived from the *Canons of Edgar*, V Atr.

[1] = *placita* in the source, *Pen. ps-Theodore* XXXVIII, 8. But see Commentary to this section.
[2] D has two such corrections, at *Canons* 22 and 53.
[3] See Section IV below.

These facts and the obvious difference of exemplar for D and for X suggest that X was made from the prototype—perhaps that version which Wulfstan referred to when collecting material for the Laws—and was preserved and corrected at Worcester by men familiar with the Archbishop's methods and interests. The manuscript tradition which gave rise to D developed outside the Worcester scriptorium, and although D's *Canons* escaped mutilation in the middle of the eleventh century when X's *Polity* was copied out, it remained inferior to X in its details because it was out of the control of the Worcester scribes.

3. THE LANGUAGE OF D AND X

The language of both these manuscripts has been described often enough to make treatment in great detail unnecessary; in general, those parts of the manuscripts which contain the *Canons* exhibit features detected by editors in other parts of the manuscripts, except where the shortness of the text makes it impossible to find examples of some points.[1] X is a clear example of 'classical' late West Saxon, but D has some linguistic features which perhaps point to a non-West Saxon dialect on the part of the scribe or the scriptorium, and which provide the main argument against Worcester as the place of origin: I shall deal with only these features at length, referring to other parts of D and X and to other manuscripts. Those linguistic characteristics which are of no significance as evidence for the provenance of D are only briefly illustrated.

A. *Unstressed vowels*

There are many examples in both manuscripts of the weakening of lightly stressed (mainly inflexional) syllables, and consequent confusion of orthography and reverse spellings. The examples below may suggest that D has more cases of weakening than X, but of course the text is too short for one to be sure of the implications of this.

(a) -*um* is replaced by -*on* or -*an*:
D preostan/ X preostum (*Canons* 7); gehalgodon/ gehalgodum (31); cræftan/ cræftum (51); gerihtan/ gerihtum (54).

---

[1] Recent descriptions are by J. M. Ure, *The Benedictine Office*, pp. 10, 67–70 (D and X); P. Goolden, *The Old English Apollonius of Tyre*, pp. xxvii–xxxii (D).

INTRODUCTION

(b) Verbal *-on* is replaced by *-an*:
   D scoldan/ X sceoldan (16); sculan/ sculon (54).
(c) Subjunctive plural *-en* is spelt *-an* in both manuscripts:
   D gefilstan/ X gefylstan (5); seman/ seman (7); sibbian/ sibbian (7); singan/ singan (57); cf. sceotan/ sceoton (7).
(d) *-od(e)* in the past of weak verbs of class 2 sporadically appears as *-ad(e)*:
   D folgode/ X folgade (10); unbiscopod/ unbiscopad (15); gewurðad/ gewurðod (49).
(e) *-u* appears once as *-a*:
   D geara/ X gearu (69); cf. ealascop/ ealusceop (59).
(f) The alternation D buton/ X butan is consistently observed.
(g) D bismer/ X bismor (39).
(h) D worlde/ X worulde (1); worldmanna/ woruldmanna (7). This contraction is noticed by Ure as appearing in the D version of *The Benedictine Office*.[1]

B. *Stressed vowels*

a–c are features which distinguish D from X and from other Worcester manuscripts.

(a) In X the *i*-mutation of *a*+nasal is normal Late WS. *e*, but D always has *æ*:

   D scænde/ X scende (12); wænige/ wenige (17); mængdon/ mengdon (39); gewænian/ wenian (55).

We may examine the frequency of *æ* in other parts of D. The first, and earliest, hand has only two instances, *længra* and *stænt*. The main mid-eleventh-century hand has it in all the works I have examined in the majority of cases where one would expect *e*. Of the works which are in D only, *Apollonius* has the feature (see Goolden, p. xxx): *acænde, asænd, bewænde, cæmpan, geglængde, wænde, gewændon*. Texts shared by D with other manuscripts almost invariably have *æ* in D for *e* in the other manuscripts. Napier I, the first text in this part of D, has *acænnede/ acende* (twice); *cænne/ cenne* as against Hatton 113 and Tiberius A xiii. Homily VI has *stæmne/ stemne (stefne); gegræmedon/ gegremedon; sænt/ sent; gebænde* (with Bodley 343)/ *gebende; asænde/ asende*: Bodley 343, C.C.C.C. 419, and Hatton 113 agree, except in the

[1] *Benedictine Office*, p. 69.

one case indicated, against D. In Homily XIX, D has *sænde/ sende* (twice); *geswænceð/ (ge)swenceð*; *gescændað/ (geswencað)*; *gegræmedon/ (ge)gremedon* as against MSS. Nero A. i and X. The versions of *Polity* in D and X agree in only one case where we would normally expect *æ* in D: *stent/ stent*; elsewhere we have (e.g.) *wændan/ wendan*; *græmiað/ gremiað*; *glængdon/ glengdan*; *rænce/ rence*; *unwæmme/ unwemme*. In cases where an extract from *Polity* occurs twice in D, the two passages agree on *æ*; where X and Nero A. i coincide, they agree on *e*. V Atr. in D and Nero A. i has *gewænde/ gewende*.

Ælfric II has *geglæncan/ glencgan*; *besæncan/ besencan*; *lændena/ lendena* (4 times); *acwænced* (with Bodley 343)/ *acwenced*; *acænnedan/ acennedan*; *awændan/ awendan*; *æftergængan/ aftergengan*; *ræmmas/ hremmas, remnæs*; *cæmpa*; *gegæncge*; *bænde*. D has *æ* in all cases where C.C.C.C. 190 and Bodley 343 have *e*, except once, as indicated; in addition, words in D only have *æ*. *The Benedictine Office*, like *Canons* in being in both D and X, has *æ* in D, *e* in X (cf. Ure, pp. 67-8): *unwæmme/ unwemme*; *besæncte/ besencte*; *adræncte/ adrencte*.

Thus the main hand of D has *æ* almost without variation in every place where other manuscripts, chiefly Worcester manuscripts, have *e*. It has *æ* in texts and words which are in D only; in texts by Wulfstan or not by Wulfstan. It must be a feature of the scribe or of the scriptorium, not of the exemplars, because the exemplars must have been many in number, and some possibly from Worcester.

That it is a feature of scriptorium rather than scribe alone is suggested by its being found in the other main mid-eleventh-century hand, that which wrote part of a translation of Genesis on pp. 151-60; although this is complicated by the fact that the burnt MS. Otho B. x contains this feature in the same extract, presumably from the same exemplar. That it is a feature of the scriptorium in which the main part of D was written is suggested by the fact that it is found only twice in the earlier part of the manuscript.

In the examples given above, *e* was found to be a feature of the Worcester manuscripts where D has *æ*; we may now look specifically for *æ/e* in the Worcester manuscripts only. Hatton 113, a Worcester manuscript closely associated with X, seems to have been designed as a companion volume to X: this is indicated by the continuity of quire-signatures, the similarity of script, and the fact that the contents of the volumes are complementary—one is

INTRODUCTION

homiletic, the other canonistic. In it, Homily XIII has *forstent, gemencged, gremiað*; III has *leng, swencað, sendeð, asendeð, gemencged*; IV has *awendan, unwrenca*; V *gemæncged, bendas, gehende, leng, lotwrencum, besenceð, gegenge*. Napier XXIX, in Hatton 113 only, has *geþencan, stent, gemencgað, wendað, unstenca, wendon*.

The *Penitential of pseudo-Ecgbert*, in Laud Misc. 482, C.C.C.C. 190, and Junius 121, has only one example of *æ*: *ænde* in Laud.

It would appear that we can consider *æ* before nasals as a standard feature of both main scribes of D, whether they are copying material by Wulfstan or not; but this is almost always replaced by *e* in Worcester manuscripts, in the earlier part of C.C.C.C. 201, and in both Wulfstan and non-Wulfstan texts. *æ* does occur in Worcester manuscripts, but extremely rarely; *e* is much more common. It may be that the original collection of texts in C.C.C.C. 201, first written in a dialect not unlike that of the undoubted Worcester manuscripts, was a generation or two later completed by two separate scribes, both of whom have this striking non-Worcester characteristic; or that the manuscript was, in the meantime, moved to another dialect area. We know too little about the movement of scribes and manuscripts in the Anglo-Saxon period to decide between these alternatives.

æ as the *i*-mutation of *a*+nasal is one of the most frequently discussed linguistic features of D.[1] Normally the *æ* produced by mutation was raised to *e* in WS., and the consistent survival of *æ* in D has been taken as evidence against a Worcester origin, or at least against a WS. scribe. On the basis of the evidence above, it appears that this is true. Our difficulty remains that of associating *æ* with a particular dialect area outside Worcester.

Raising of *æ* to *e* did not take place in Essex, *æ* (+*n*) becoming *a* in ME.; Goolden (p. xxxi) confidently states 'it can therefore be assumed without serious doubt that these *æ* forms are the work of an Essex scribe who introduced dialect forms into a West Saxon copy'. Fehr, on the other hand, refers to Bülbring (*Altenglisches Elementarbuch*, para. 171), who speaks of 'südöstlichen Patois', and then (*Hirtenbriefe*, p. xvi) assigns the manuscript to Canterbury.[2]

---

[1] Schlemilch, *Beiträge*, p. xxxiv; Fehr, *Hirtenbriefe*, pp. xv ff.; Goolden, p. xxx; Ure, pp. 67–8; *Sermo Lupi*, p. 43.

[2] Anyone who wished to follow up the connection of D with the south-east might note that a hint is provided by Bx. The text printed in Appendix II, reflecting passages of *NPL* and *Canons*, was added to the commonplace-book

But Luick (para. 186) considered it southern but neither pure Kentish nor WS. Ure, in whose text (*The Benedictine Office*) the opposition æ/e is consistent in D/X, does not commit himself on a decision, and we should be wise to take up this position. Bülbring comments that the feature occurs in southern areas other than the south-east. Dr. and Miss Sisam also illustrate how the feature is found in manuscripts from areas other than the south-east, and conclude: 'these examples show that æ for the mutation of *a*+nasal was not confined to OE. manuscripts from south-eastern districts, and that it was at least tolerated over a wide area of Southern England'.[1] But not, it appears, in Worcester at the time when the other major collections of Wulfstan material were being written.

(*b*) *ie* does not occur. X shows the regular development to *y*; but D prefers *i* for this and for Late WS. *y* of any origin, including *y* as the mutation of *u*. If the spelling *i* in D indicates unrounding, then it is difficult to accept it as a Worcester manuscript, for the development in that area is definitely from *y* to a rounded sound later represented by *u*.

The distribution of *i*/*y* is very like that of æ(+*n*)/*e*(+*n*): that is to say, D has *i* in both Wulfstan and non-Wulfstan material, whereas X and other Worcester manuscripts have *y*. However, *i* for *y*, unlike æ for *e*, is not an invariable rule. In the *Canons*: *gefilstan*/ *gefylstan* (5); *gehwilc*/ *gehwylc*; *scriftscire*/ *scriftscyre* (6); *gif*/ *gyf* (7); *gebirige*/ *gebyrige* (twice, 9); *gildscipe*/ *gyldscipe* (9); *gebirda*/ *gebyrda* (13); *gitsigende*/ *gytsiende* (14); *gehwilce*/ *gehwylce*; *tiðege*/ *tyðige*; *girne*/ *gyrne* (15); *wilweorþunga*/ *wyllweorðunga* (16); *dislicra*/ *dyslicra* (20), etc. As for non-Wulfstan texts in D, Goolden (p. xxviii) notices the presence of *i* in *Apollonius*: *swiðe*, *micele*, *gewilnunge*, *swilce*, *scilde*, *hi*, *hire* (but *hyre* frequently), *andwirde*, *girnde*. Ure (p. 68) picks out *i*/*y* in the D/X versions of *The Benedictine Office*, and there is no need to add to his examples. I take further instances from *Polity* in D and X: *gebirað*/ *gebyreþ*; *swiþe*/ *swyðe*; *ifele*/ *yfele*; *sixte*/ *syxte*; *þisum þrim*/ *þyssum ðrym*; *scilfð*/ *scylfð* (but *scylfð*/ *scylfð* later); *filigan*/ *fyligean*, etc. The scribes of Hatton 113, Nero A. i, and the earlier part of D all prefer *y*, although *i* is by no means impossible to find.

(*c*) A third feature which distinguishes D is the choice of simple

---

MS. Bx, originally of a conventional WS. dialect, in a clear south-eastern dialect in the early twelfth century.

[1] The Salisbury Psalter, E.E.T.S. 242 (1959), p. 14.

INTRODUCTION

back vowels after *sc*-. The position is like that with regard to *i*/*y*: D prefers simple vowels, but does not use them exclusively; X and the Worcester manuscripts show a marked preference for diphthongal spellings. In the *Canons* we have: *biscop*/ *bisceop* (5); *scoldan*/ *sceoldan* (16); *scare*/ *sceare* (47); *ealascop*/ *ealusceop* (59); *biscop* (D70); but *sceotan*/ *sceoton* (7); Ure and Goolden do not note this feature in their texts, where in fact the relevant contexts are rare. *The Benedictine Office* has D *sceope*/ X *sceope*; *scoldan*/ *sceoldan*; *gescop*/ *gesceop*. *Apollonius* has only *scamfæst*, *scame*, *scolde*. *Polity* has *biscopas*/ *bisceopas* (frequently); *þeodscaðan*/ *þeodsceaðan* (twice); *scoldan*/ *sceoldan*; *scolde*/ *sceolde*, etc.

However, this contrast seems to be a less reliable distinguishing feature than (*a*) or (*b*). The simple vowel spelling is found, sometimes consistently, in some texts in Worcester manuscripts, and our opposition D/Worcester manuscripts needs to be modified. Although C.C.C.C. 419 and Bodley 343 agree on *eo*, *ea* in the *Sermo Lupi*, whereas D has *o* and *a*, Hatton 113 and Nero A. i have about twenty examples of *o* or *a*. Homily II, in D and Hatton 113 (E), has D *scolde*/ E *sceolde*; *scolde*/ *sceolde*; *scolde*/ *scolde*; *scoldon*/ *sceoldan*; *scoldan*/ *scoldan*; Homily III provides two examples of *scoldan* (*-on*) in both these manuscripts, and none of *sceo-*. IV has (*sculon*)/ *sceolan* and *earmscapenan*/ *earmsceapenan*. V in E has *biscope*, *scoldan*, *þeodscaðan*, demonstrating that occurrences of the simple vowels are not restricted to *scold(on)* in the Worcester manuscripts, as might at first appear. VI in E has *biscopas*, *gesceop* (twice), *gescop* (four times), *scoldan* (three times), *gescapen* (twice), *scolde* (three times), *sceolde*.

It thus appears that, whereas D's choice of an *o* or *a* after *sc-* is fairly consistent, E especially among the Worcester manuscripts is not so consistent in its choice of *eo* or *ea*. If we are to argue the non-Worcester origin of D on the basis of its linguistic characteristics, we must leave (*c*) out of account.

D appears not to come from Worcester, or at least not to be the product of scribes trained at Worcester. We cannot locate the manuscript precisely on the evidence provided by present linguistic knowledge. *æ* points vaguely to a southern as opposed to northern origin, despite the presence of *NPL* in the manuscript. There are no clear and consistent Anglian features.[1] We cannot be more

---

[1] There is only the failure of breaking, in *galdra*, and this is a conventional spelling; X6 has *befallen*.

precise than this, in the present state of our knowledge of OE. regional spelling conventions.

(d) The group *weor-*. Ure cites several D forms *wur-* and X forms *weor-* and *wyr-* from *The Benedictine Office*. There appears to be no consistent distinction, however, and, as Ure points out, 'Worcester texts have both *weor-* and *wur-*' (p. 68; cf. *Sermo Lupi*, p. 40). In the *Canons* we find D *wurðige/* X *wurðie* (2); *wurðe/ wyrðe* (15); *wyrðe/ wyrðe* (22); *weorðfull/ weorðfull* (59), etc.

(e) *a/o* before nasals is always *a* in both D and X.

(f) In most cases, D has *-nesse*, X *-nysse*: *gerædnessum* (D3); *arwurðnesse/ arwyrðnysse* (26); *oferseocnesse/ oferseocnysse* (36); *clænnesse/ clænnysse* (38); but *oferseocnesse/ oferseocnesse* (30).

c. *Consonants*

Another well-known feature of D is its loss of *h-* before *r*. It is consistent through the manuscript, but there is only one opportunity for an example in the *Canons*: *ringe/ hrincge* (45).[1]

The second hand of the mid-eleventh-century part of D, which wrote out a translation of part of Genesis, has *u-* for *f-* regularly. Professor Whitelock informs me that it is not found in the Genesis extract in Otho B. x; and it does not occur in the main hand of D.

II. AUTHORSHIP AND DATE

To some extent, the *Canons of Edgar* looks back to periods earlier than the eleventh century. Many of its regulations are aimed at correcting evils in the life of churchmen which had been criticized in the eighth century by Bede and Boniface, and later Alcuin, and a similar purpose is revealed in the decrees of the Synod of Clovesho in 747. But a more obvious context for the work is the tenth and early eleventh century, when the Benedictine reformation was at its height. Dunstan and Edgar were in the van of the reform movement in this period, and it seemed appropriate to nineteenth-century historians to date the *Canons* in the reign of Edgar, especially with the evidence of the rubric to D to support them.[2] Stubbs without hesitation attributed the work to Dunstan, giving the entirely impressionistic view that one or two of the regulations

[1] For other examples see Ure, p. 69; Goolden, p. xxix.
[2] See discussion, p. 22, below.

were 'especially characteristic' of the saint.¹ Böhmer and Oakley were less willing to credit Dunstan with the *Canons*, although they claimed that it was the product of an unknown canonist of the time of Edgar. Liebermann called it 'ein wahrscheinlich erst nach Eadgar ... entstandenes Denkmal'.²

There are two pieces of internal evidence which appear to support these attributions. The heading on p. 97 of D reads

HER GEBIRAÐ NU TO EADGARES. GERÆDNES. BE GEHADODRA MANNA LIFFADUNGE.

At *Canons* 68c there is a passage in X only which begins

Dunstan gedemde þæt ...

The nineteenth-century attributions are untenable for two reasons, apart from the fact that the work can now be confidently attributed to a particular eleventh-century author. First, although the set of rules is consistent with Dunstan's reforming intention, there is no evidence apart from that of *Canons* 68c to connect him with the *Canons*, no hint that he left anything which can be identified with the *Canons*. Second, the authority of the manuscripts is unacceptable. As will be seen,³ the passage in X which contains the reference to Dunstan was probably not in the original, and it does not occur in D. Likewise the claim in D that the regulations were issued by Edgar is absent from X, where the title is replaced by ITEM SINODALIA DECRETA. No completely convincing explanation of the mention of Edgar has yet been made, but as we have no other grounds for crediting him with the work, and can reasonably attribute it to Wulfstan, we must believe that either Wulfstan or a later scribe wished to give authority to the work by fathering it on Edgar.

Jost's article of 1932⁴ demonstrated that the *Canons* must be dated between 1004–6 and 1008, because of its relationship with datable sources and dependent texts. The *terminus a quo* is provided by Ælfric's *Pastoral Letters*, to which the *Canons* is heavily indebted.⁵ *Canons* 14 proves beyond question that the *Pastoral Letter*

---

[1] W. Stubbs, *Memorials of St. Dunstan*, Rolls Series 63 (1874), cvii.
[2] *Gesetze* III, 221.
[3] See Commentary under *Canons* 62.
[4] 'Einige Wulfstantexte und ihre Quellen', *Anglia*, lvi (1932), pp. 265–315.
[5] See Section III, below.

to *Wulfsige* (Ælfric I, probably the first in order of composition) was used:

Ælfric I, 77: Ne preost ne beo magnere ne gitsigende massere.

Canons 14: And we læraŏ þæt preosta gehwilc tilige him rihtlice, and ne beo ænig mangere mid unrihte ne gitsigende massere.

It can be proved on stylistic grounds that the author of the *Canons* was the borrower. If Wulfstan was its author, then the alterations made to the *Pastoral Letter* are typical of the way he rewrote sources, and are designed to bring the derived work into line with his normal style. Jost illustrated how the phrase *mid unrihte* was a characteristic addition of Wulfstan's.[1] It should also be noted that the rhythm of *Canons* 14 is closer than that of Ælfric I, 77 to that associated with Wulfstan.[2] It seems most likely that it is Ælfric who has been subjected to revision.

The *terminus a quo*, is, therefore, to be decided by reference to the dates of Ælfric's *Pastoral Letters*, the closest chronologically of Wulfstan's sources.[3] The latest date which can be proposed for the composition of Ælfric I is 1002, the end of Wulfsige's episcopacy. In fact, Clemoes (p. 244) places it rather early in the set of texts which he dates 992–1002. As it can be proved that the *Canons* also borrows from the *Pastoral Letters* which follow Ælfric I, and which were addressed to Wulfstan, our text cannot be dated too close to 1002. Clemoes dates Ælfric 2a late in the period 1002–5; 2 and 3 in 1005; II and III in 1006. II, 161–2 provide the exact content of *Canons* 41; III, 80 provides the closest parallel to *Canons* 51. The *terminus a quo* must be 1006, or, if the one parallel each from II and III is not thought convincing, 1005–6.

The *terminus ad quem* can be fixed more easily: *Canons* 19, 24, and 54 provide material for sections 13. 1, 18 and 11–11. 1 of Ethelred's fifth legal code, which was issued at Enham in 1008.[4]

If we date the *Canons* 1005–7 on the basis of the evidence presented above, then it was compiled during Wulfstan's writing career. Despite the *Dictionary of National Biography*, all Wulfstan scholars would agree that he was Bishop of London in 996, Arch-

---

[1] 'Einige Wulfstantexte', pp. 294–7.

[2] See A. McIntosh, 'Wulfstan's Prose', *Proceedings of the British Academy*, xxxv (1949), 109–42.

[3] See discussion in B. Fehr, *Hirtenbriefe*, xxxv–lii, and P. Clemoes, 'The Chronology of Ælfric's Works', *The Anglo-Saxons*, pp. 212–47.

[4] *Gesetze* I, 246–59. See K. Sisam, *Studies in the History of Old English Literature* (Oxford, 1953), Note A, pp. 278–87.

bishop of York and Bishop of Worcester in 1002. He held the Worcester see until 1016, and the archbishopric until his death in 1023.[1] Even allowing for the uncertainty of the *terminus a quo*, the *Canons* still falls within Wulfstan's lifetime and his writing career. The dating 1005–7 would agree well with the rough relative chronology which has been suggested for his works. Professor Bethurum believes that the group of eschatological homilies—II, III, Ia, Ib, IV, and V in her edition—came first, in the order listed.[2] These are probably the outcome of Wulfstan's early concern about Christian morals, and are to be associated with his feelings on the millennium, which would have been particularly strong just before and after the turn of the century, while he was Bishop of London, and in the early days of his episcopacy at Worcester and York. Next Bethurum places a group of homilies of practical instruction, in the order Xa, VI, VII, IX, XI, VIIIa, VIIIb, Xb, Xc, and VIIIc. The sequence of these pieces, and the fact that they were, like the *Canons*, written before V Atr., can be established on the grounds of mutual borrowings.[3] There is less certainty about the position of the other homilies, XIII–XXI, but they probably came after[4] the second group, which she calls 'The Christian Faith'.

The *Canons of Edgar* is related to this second group both in intention and content. Its date of composition coincides exactly with the period in which Wulfstan was writing homilies with a similar purpose—to instruct his priests how to serve God and how to teach their people in the manner best suited to stem the decline of morals. This is the period of instruction, and in it the written works contrast with the works of the earlier and later periods of exhortation, represented, for example, by Homily III and the *Sermo Lupi ad Anglos* respectively. Both the *Canons* and the 'Christian Faith' homilies agree in being the work of a reforming bishop engaged on a practical campaign; Wulfstan is the great example of this type of ecclesiastic in the early years of eleventh-century England.[5]

This general impression of the *Canons* as particularly suited to the hand of Wulfstan in the first decade of the eleventh century is

[1] The most useful accounts of Wulfstan's life are D. Whitelock, *Sermo Lupi*, pp. 7–17, and 'A Note on the Career of Wulfstan the Homilist', *E.H.R.* lii (1937), 460–5.
[2] *Homilies*, p. 103.
[3] Ibid., pp. 103, 299–307.
[4] Except XIV and XV, which Professor Bethurum thinks are early.
[5] See below, Chapter IV.

confirmed by connections of detail with the homilies of instruction. It borrows from the *Regula Canonicorum* group (ch. 145 of Amalarius of Metz, Wulfstan's translation, homily Xa, and his later adaptation, homily Xc) in the following sections:

Borrowing of ideas: *Can.* 11, 22, 53.
Similarities of phrasing: *Can.* 1, 2, 8, 13, 17, 61.

The material from the *Canons* which reappears in Homily VIIIc and V Atr. also testifies to the close connection between our text and Wulfstan's other writings of the same period.[1]

All the parallel passages are set out in the Commentary. In this place it will be sufficient to quote two examples which connect the *Canons* with the 'Christian Faith' group.

Can. 1 (X): and þæt heo beon heora woruldhlafordum eac holde and getrywe æfter Godes rihte.
from Xc, 165–6: Beo manna gehwylc hold 7 getrywe his worldhlaforde æfre mid rihte.

Can. 61: And we lærað þæt ænig preost ne lufige wifmanna neawyste ealles to swiðe, ac lufige his rihtæwe, þæt is his cirice.
from Xa, 33–4: Forbugan hi a wifmanna neaweste swa hi æfre geornost magon.
+Xa, 11–13: Ne beon hi ... æwbrecan, ac healdan heora riht æwe, þæt is heora mynster.

In addition to the specific borrowings which the *Canons* makes from *Be Cristendome* (Xc), there is a general correspondence between the teachings of the two works, and a concern with the same subjects. In one passage of *Be Cristendome* there are compressed a number of points which Wulfstan elaborates in the *Canons*:

Xc, 102–9:
Ne ænig man ne sy to sacfull ne ealles to geflitgeorn (*Can.* 7, 23). Ne ænig man ne lufige druncen to swyðe ne fule oferfylle (*Can.* 58–9). Ne ænig man myrtenes æfre ne abite ne blodes ne abyrige (*Can.* 53). Ne ænig man wiccecræft æfre begange. Ne ænig man idola weorðie æfre (*Can.* 16). ... Sunnandæges weorðunge nænig man forgyme (*Can.* 19, 52). Ælc man his teoðunga gelæste mid rihte (54). Freolsa 7 fæstena healde man georne (*Can.* 18, 23–5, 49).

This passage in particular, and the content of the 'Christian Faith' group of homilies in general, evince the same interests as

[1] See Commentary under *Canons* 16, 17, 22 (VIIIc); 19, 24, 54 (V Atr.).

the *Canons*. The many connections of detail, and the coincidence of dates of composition, make it unlikely that the *Canons of Edgar* and the homilies in question were not written by the same man. The resemblance of the *Canons* to *Be Cristendome* is particularly striking, and it seems likely that this homily was written by Wulfstan not long before he wrote the *Canons*.

From the time of Wanley to the present day it has been accepted that Wulfstan had a characteristic style which could be analysed and used as a norm for testing authorship. The typical features have been listed many times, and there is no need to justify the method by enumerating them here.[1] The *Canons*, which have not before been studied from this point of view, exhibit most of the characteristics of Wulfstan's style, for example:

Intensifying adverbs and adverbial phrases:
   georne: 28, 34, 38 (twice), 45, 49, 57, 58, 60, 68, 69.
   geornlice: 1, 16, 17, 51.
   swiðe: 42 (twice), 60.
   ealles to swiðe: 61, D23.
   aa: 52.
   mid rihte: 22.
   mid unrihte: 14.
   mid ealle: 16.

There is a high incidence of phrases which consist of alliterating pairs of words, often roughly synonymous:

   holde and gehyrsume: 1.
   æt freolsan and æt fæstenan: 48.
   wis and weorðfull: 59.

The following dual phrases occur elsewhere in Wulfstan:

   þeowigende and þenigende: 1.
   Ben. Off., p. 81, 16–17: þeowian *and* ðenian.
   Hom. Xa 8: þeowian *and* ðenian.
         47: ðeowian *and* ðenian.

---

[1] For a convenient account of Wulfstan's style, see Bethurum, *Homilies*, pp. 87–8; on pp. 24–49 she shows in detail how stylistic tests have been used to arrive at the canon.
Other studies are to be found in J. P. Kinard, *A Study of Wulfstan's Homilies* (Baltimore, 1897), pp. 19–32; Jost, *Wulfstanstudien*, pp. 155–61 (on vocabulary and syntax); Ure, *The Benedictine Office*, pp. 30–9; Fowler, 'Some Stylistic Features of the *Sermo Lupi*', *J.E.G.Ph.* lxv (1966), 1–18.

holde and getrywe: 1.
Hom. Xc, 165–6: hold 7 getrywe.

ge for Gode ge for worlde: 1.
Sermo Lupi, 72: for Gode 7 for worolde.[1]

lufian and læran: 2.
Hom. Xc, 169–70: lufie 7 lære.
           177: lufian 7 læran.

seman and sibbian: 7.
Hom. Xa, 23; XIII, 63–4: sibbe 7 some.

bodigan and aa wel bisnian: 52.
ge wel bodige ge wel bisnige: 69.
II *Polity* 60: hi scylan bodian *and* bisnian georne.
     103: ge wel bodian ge wel bysnian.[2]

Wulfstan's habitual arrangement of words and word-groups in pairs was, as Professor McIntosh has demonstrated, aimed at producing the peculiar two-stress rhythmical pattern which is the basis of his style.[3] Each syntactic phrase in a piece of continuous prose is a two-stress rhythmical unit. The functionally important words—nouns, verbs, adjectives, adverbs—carry main stress, while the less important words—prepositions, pronouns, and connectives—bear secondary stress, which is not rhythmically so important. According to McIntosh's scheme, there are only these two kinds of sentence stress, with no intermediate degrees. The heavily stressed words are arranged into pairs, largely by the syntax, and the relatively lightly stressed elements serve to space the main stresses. The normal 'foot' consists of two stresses; a number of sub-types can be distinguished by describing the metrical units in terms of the distribution of the two stressed syllables, and the number of lightly stressed syllables which precede, divide, and follow them. The wide range of variation can be seen from these two examples from the *Canons*; McIntosh's system of notation is used to show the rhythm:

$$\overset{\prime\ \ \ \ \ \ \ \ \ \ \times\ \ \ \ \ \ \ \ \ \prime\ \ \ \ \ \ \times}{\text{wis and weorðfull:}}\ 59$$

$$\overset{\prime\ \ \times\ \ \times\times\times\ \ \times\ \ \ \prime\ \ \ \ \times\ \ \ \ \times\ \ \times}{\text{mæssepreosta oððe mynsterpreosta:}}\ 46$$

---

[1] This tag is, of course, not limited in occurrence to Wulfstan's work; but it is a special favourite of his.

[2] This phrase occurs many times in *Polity*.

[3] McIntosh, op. cit.; cf. O. Funke, 'Some Remarks on Wulfstan's Prose Rhythm', *English Studies*, xliii (1962), 311–18.

INTRODUCTION xxxiii

Much of the *Canons* can be analysed into these two-stress rhythmical units; but it is not rhythmically so 'typical' as some of the prose, and the reason for this is easy to find. The work consists of a number of short sections, each made to conform to a common formula; under these conditions we cannot expect to find the marked continuous rhythm which characterizes the longer prose passages of the homilies. Because of the formulaic nature of the *Canons*, it is impossible to draw up statistics for the incidence of particular patterns for comparison with McIntosh's statistical analysis of some of the homilies; but in much of the *Canons* the rhythm is clear enough, and the rhythmical passages sufficiently integrated, to allow us to detect the hand of Wulfstan.

The *Canons of Edgar* also contains many instances of the sentence- and phrase-parallelism which is a prominent feature of Wulfstan's prose: that is to say, 'balance' of the type used, for example, by Lyly, involving longer segments than the word-pairs quoted on pp. xxxi–ii, above. Three examples from the early part of the *Canons* illustrate this well; I have marked the main stresses and the divisions between units:

/ hǽþenra léoða / and déofles gámena /: 18.
/ bécc and réaf / to gódcundre þénunge / and blǽc and bócfel / to héora gerǽdnessum /: 3.
/ þæt man fréolsdagum and fǽstendagum / forga áðas and órdela /: 24.

Two sentences from *Be Cristendome* show how Wulfstan used this form of rhetoric in the homilies:

Dómas 7 díhtas / ríhte man géornlice, / þæt léod 7 lágu / trúmlice stánde / (164–5).
/ Sé þe wǽre gífre, / wéorðe se sýfre; / (124: this pattern is repeated through several lines).

The word-lists which are so common in the *Sermo Lupi* and the eschatological homilies are represented in the *Canons* only by a short list in 16; again, the formulaic nature of the work is against this form of rhetoric.

wyllweorðunga, and licwigelunga, and hwata, and galdra, and treowwurðunga, and stanwurðunga: X16.

This examination of the style of the *Canons of Edgar* shows that the text exhibits features which are thought to be highly characteristic of Wulfstan. To this evidence, and that of the close relationship between the *Canons* and the 'Christian Faith' group of homilies, may be added hints given by the manuscripts. Of the two manuscripts in which the complete work appears, one is definitely a Worcester manuscript. D may not be a Worcester manuscript, but its contents associate it closely with Wulfstan. Both X and D contain some of Wulfstan's own writings, and his principal sources. The presence of the *Canons* in these manuscripts, one of which was written at Worcester and both of which contain so much Wulfstan material, strongly confirms the impression of Wulfstan's authorship given by the internal evidence outlined in the preceding pages.

The connection of the *Canons* with Ælfric also points to the same conclusion. Wulfstan knew the *Pastoral Letter to Wulfsige*, whose episcopacy at Sherborne ended the year Wulfstan went to Worcester, and it may have been his admiration for this which prompted him to make a request to Ælfric for further information on pastoral duties and conduct. Ælfric I is a standard work in Wulfstan's 'commonplace-book'.[1] The other *Pastoral Letters* were written for Wulfstan, and it is reasonable to assume that their recipient was the man who, almost immediately after their composition, used them to provide the basis of his own work on the conduct of priests, the *Canons of Edgar*.

III. SOURCES

Reference to the *Commentary* will reveal that there is little in the *Canons of Edgar* for which parallels cannot be found in Wulfstan's own work or elsewhere. Wulfstan subscribed to the medieval respect for authority in excerpting from the sources which were held in best esteem in his time. He had greater reason for doing this for the *Canons* than for the homilies, because the *Canons* is intended as a set of official rules binding for his clergy; there is little room for arbitrary pronouncements of his own, and the work gains weight by the backing of recognized authorities. Here Wulfstan is the mouthpiece of Church tradition, original only in assembling directions on a wide range of questions of clerical and lay practice and in rephrasing his sources in his own manner. The result is that while hardly one of the ideas is strictly his own, the work bears the stamp of his editorship.

[1] See D. Bethurum, 'Archbishop Wulfstan's Commonplace Book', *P.M.L.A.* lvii (1942), and Section IV, below.

Four works have been used extensively: the *Capitula* of Theodulf of Orleans;[1] Ælfric's *Pastoral Letters*;[2] the *Excerptiones pseudo-Ecgberti*;[3] and the *Homilia*[4] of Leo IV (Pope, 847–55). Other sources, somewhat less extensively used, are chapter 145 of Amalarius of Metz's *De Regula Canonicorum* (via Wulfstan's translation, Homily Xa, and his later adaptation, *Be Cristendome*, Xc), the spurious *Penitential of Theodore*,[5] and the *Penitential of pseudo-Ecgbert*.[6] All the parallel passages are set out in full in the Commentary, and I discuss in this section only those passages which prove Wulfstan's direct knowledge of the most important sources. The following criteria have been used to determine such direct knowledge.

Verbal similarity is naturally much stronger in the case of dependence on OE. sources, but a similarity of phrasing to a Latin source can often be detected, and the inclusion of unimportant ideas in a passage, or the arrangement of ideas in the same sequence as in the suspected source, are frequently significant. Where no verbal connection exists, the contexts of the parallels have been taken into consideration. Sometimes successive regulations in the source are reproduced in the same order, or in proximity, in the *Canons*, and this continuity reinforces a judgement based on correspondence of ideas.

Broadly speaking, an article from the *Canons* may be referred to its suspected source when other parts of this source are used in a number of passages in the *Canons*, whereas the use of a source which is paralleled only once in the *Canons*, and with no verbal similarity, is difficult to prove. Greater weight is lent if the source is a well-known work of wide manuscript circulation.

For several regulations in the *Canons* more than one source is quoted. I have normally given an opinion on which one is nearest to the *Canons*, but it must be stressed that, where the sources concerned are habitual, there is no necessity to take an absolute decision (even if it were possible); it is highly probable that Wulfstan had more than one in mind, and the existence of his 'commonplace-

---

[1] Ed. Migne, *PL* cv. 191–208.
[2] Ed. B. Fehr, *Die Hirtenbriefe Ælfrics*.
[3] Ed. B. Thorpe, *Ancient Laws* (folio ed., 1840), pp. 326–42.
[4] Ed. Migne, *PL* cxv. 675–83.   [5] *Ancient Laws*, 277–306.
[6] Ed. J. Raith, *Die altenglische Version des Halitgar'schen Bussbuches*, Bibliothek der angelsächsischen Prosa, xiii (Hamburg, 1933). Jost, *Polity*, pp. 178–209, cites some minor sources in addition to these; these are noted in my Commentary.

book' (see Section IV) would have made reference to a number of sources easy.

The Capitula of Theodulf

Theodulf of Orleans was just the type of reformer to find favour with Wulfstan, who made extensive use of his *Capitula* and *Liber de ordine baptismi* in the homilies. The *Capitula*, upon which Wulfstan drew in the present work, exists, in its Latin version, in two manuscripts of the eleventh century.[1] In addition to this, there are two separate OE. versions. An extremely literal translation is found in MS. Bodley 865 (2737), ff. 89–112.[2] As this begins imperfect at Chapter 25, it is practically useless for comparison with the *Canons*, where Wulfstan draws on the earlier chapters of the *Capitula*. A complete, and distinct, translation occurs in C.C.C.C. 201, pp. 231–69.[3] It was not originally a part of D, but was earlier bound with C.C.C.C. 191, an Exeter manuscript of the *Bilingual Rule of Chrodegang*.[4] In view of this fact we cannot assume that Wulfstan knew the OE. version simply because it now occurs in a manuscript obviously connected with him.

His indebtedness to the *Capitula* is very great. The corresponding passages are as follows:

Definite sources: *Canons* D3–4: *Capitula* IV; 9: XIV; 10: XV; 22: XXII; 23: XLII; 25: XLIII; 29: IX; 43: V; 44: VI; 49: XXXVIII; 58: XIII.

Additional parallels and doubtful cases: 11: III; 26: X; 30: XI; 35: VII.

The relationship between these parallel passages rarely involves a similarity of wording; but the cumulative effect of so many regulations which are to be found in Theodulf, often included in the *Canons* in the same sequence, vouches for the authenticity of individual sections. A comparison of *Canons* 3–4 with their source, *Capitula* IV, illustrates the nature of the relationship:

Can. 3. And we lærað þæt hi to ælcon sinoðe habban ælce geare becc and reaf to godcundre þenunge, and blæc and bocfel to heora geræpdnessum, and þreora daga biwiste.

---

[1] C.C.C.C. 201 (not D: Ker no. 50) and C.C.C.C. 265.
[2] Ed. A. S. Napier, *The ... Enlarged Rule of Chrodegang, together with an OE. version ... of the 'Capitula' of Theodulf* (E.E.T.S., o.s. 150, 1916).
[3] Ed. *Ancient Laws*, 466–88, as 'Ecclesiastical Institutes'.
[4] See Ker, *Catalogue*, pp. 74–5, 91.

4. And we læraðþæt preosta gehwilc to sinoðe hæbbe his cleric and gefædne man to cnihte, and nænigne unwitan þe disig lufige; ac faran ealle mid gefæde and mid Godes ælmihtiges ege.

Capitula IV. Quando more solito ad synodum convenitis, vestimenta, et libros, et vasa sancta, cum quibus vestrum ministerium et injunctum officium peragitis, vobiscum deferte; nec non duos, aut tres clericos, cum quibus missarum solemnia celebratis, vobiscum adducite, ut probetur quam diligenter, quam studiose Dei servitium peragatis.

OE. *Capitula* IV. Ðæm tydum þe ge bisceopa gemot secen. habbað eow mid swylc mæsse-reaf. 7 swylce bec. 7 swylce husel-fata. 7 swylce ge mid risnum eow þa befæstan þenunga þenian magon. 7 .ii. preostas oððe .iii. oþþe swa fela læwedra to þæm gecydra. þæt hi þæt haliȝe geryne arwurðlice mid eow breman mægen. þæt mon on eow geseon mæge hu geornlice 7 hu hihtlice ge Gode on eowrum þenungum þeowien.

Whilst it is certain that the *Capitula* provides the source for this passage, it is not possible to tell whether the Latin or the OE. version is the immediate source. This is the case in most places where the *Capitula* lies behind a section of the *Canons*: the OE. *Capitula* is usually so literal a translation, and its relationship with the *Canons* so frequently non-verbal, that it is no closer to the *Canons* than its Latin original. This is perhaps surprising, as Wulfstan usually adopted the basic wording of his OE. sources quite faithfully, merely adding his own embellishments: as, for example, in the revision in D of Ælfric II. But there is evidence that he sometimes commissioned literal OE. translations of Latin works and then rewrote them completely: this is Professor Bethurum's interpretation of the OE. translation of Abbo of St. Germain's *Sermo in Cena Domini ad Penitentes* which appears in C.C.C.C. 190, and which is used by Wulfstan in his own *Sermo de Cena Domini* (XV).[1] The OE. *Capitula* may stand in a similar relation to the *Canons*.

Although there is a general lack of correspondence of detail between the OE. *Capitula* and the *Canons*, two passages may show that the translation was known to Wulfstan and used by him in the *Canons*.

Can. 29: . . . bute man wite þæt he on life Gode to ðam wel gecweme . . .

[1] Bethurum, *Homilies*, p. 346.

The phrase *bute man wite* appears to be derived from *þæt mon wite* in a similar context in the OE. *Capitula* IX; it has no counterpart in the Latin.

> *Can.* 22: ... he ne bið wel cristen ...

OE. *Capitula* XXII has a very similar wording, *ne mæg he beon wel cristen*, from the Latin *catholicus esse non poterit*.[1] This borrowing is complicated by the appearance of the phrase in two other places: as *he ne bið wel cristen* in Homily VIIIc, 148, and in an entirely different context as *se byð wel cristen* in Homily VII, 171. Its occurrence in VIIIc is easily explained, as this homily was written after the *Canons* and quotes from it several times. But VII is usually dated before the *Canons*, whereas *se byð wel cristen* sounds like an imperfect recollection, i.e. a later version, of the phrase in *Canons* 22 and OE. *Capitula* XXII. The matter is discussed further in the Commentary; for the present, it is sufficient to say that the use of the phrase in Homily VII gives further evidence of Wulfstan's knowledge of the OE. *Capitula*, and perhaps indicates that he consulted it at a stage earlier than the composition of the *Canons of Edgar*.[2]

In summarizing the question of the contribution of Theodulf's *Capitula*, one can say that the debt of the *Canons* to this work was fundamental: it is highly probable that twelve articles at least were based on it. There is some evidence that the OE. translation now bound with D was referred to during the compilation of the *Canons*, but there is no internal evidence at all which would lead us to prefer the Latin to the OE. as the source of any particular passage. On the other hand, in ten out of the twelve parallel passages there is nothing which leads us to prefer the OE. to the Latin. It is known that, when Wulfstan had a Latin original and an OE. translation to work from, he was in the habit of consulting the Latin as well as the OE. with a view to improving his translation. Jost has demonstrated this practice in the relationship between Amalarius' *De Regula Canonicorum*, Wulfstan's translation (Xa), and the *Canons*.[3]

---

[1] Professor Whitelock has pointed out to me that *cristen*, used by the translator of the *Capitula* and by Wulfstan in all the phrases apparently derived from this source, is a less usual translation of *catholicus* than *rihtgeleafful* or some other word suggesting 'orthodox'; it may be that the contrast between Christian and heathen was more relevant at Wulfstan's period (cf. *Can.* 16) than the earlier contrast between Catholic and heterodox.

[2] Cf. Commentary under *Canons* 22, 29, and 35.

[3] See Jost, 'Einige Wulfstantexte', pp. 290–2.

We know also from Wulfstan's borrowings from the *Liber de ordine baptismi* in the series of homilies VIIIa–c that he referred direct to Theodulf's Latin. These circumstances make it clear that Wulfstan used the Latin as well as the OE. *Capitula* in compiling the *Canons*.

Ælfric's Pastoral Letters

These Latin and OE. letters, all but one of which are addressed to Wulfstan, may have given him the idea of making such a collection of regulations as the *Canons*, for the intention and range of subjects are similar in both works. Wulfstan's debt to Ælfric is considerable; it is clear that the archbishop made constant reference to the *Pastoral Letters* in his search for material. The following is a list of sections derived from Ælfric; the numbering follows that of Fehr's edition, where roman numerals are used for the OE. letters, arabic for the Latin.

Definite sources: *Canons* 8: Ælfric 2, 194–5;   14: I, 77;   15: 2, 163;   26: I, 48;   28: I, 107;   30: I, 69–70;   31: 2, 142;   34: I, 52–4;   38: I, 133–6;   40: 3, 68 and 71 *or* 2a, XI–XII;   41: II, 161–2;   45: I, 49–51;   51: III, 80;   60: I, 82;   68: I, 83–5 and others—see Commentary;   69: I, 85;   70: I, 51.

Additional parallels and doubtful cases: 8: II, 207, I, 73;   12: III, 190;   14: II, 185, 2, 171–2;   15: I, 71, II, 177;   26: I, 105–6, 3, 24–5, III, 20;   27: 3, 72, III, 115;   28: 3, 25;   30: 3, 23, III, 19;   33: I, 55, 58, 2, 140;   34: 2, 137–9, II, 157–8;   35: III, 84;   37: II, 75, 3, 73, 75;   39: 2, 140, 3, 32, II, 159, III, 70, 74;   40: III, 93–4, 97;   41: I, 58, 2, 141;   42: I, 33, II, 104;   45: 2, 62–4, II, 69–73;   51: 3, 40;   52: I, 42, I, 61, 2, 159, II, 175;   56: I, 68;   58: I, 74, 2, 173, II, 186;   59: III, 188;   60: III, 186;   61: I, 2, 16a, 2, 195;   66: I, 74–5, 2, 173–4;   68: 2, 165–8, I, 112–13.

It can be seen that the majority of the sections listed are derived from Ælfric I, the OE. *Letter to Wulfsige*. The parallel between Ælfric I, 77 and *Canons* 14 proves beyond question that Wulfstan knew and used this source:[1]

> Ælfric I, 77: Ne preost ne beo mangere ne gitsigende massere.
> *Can.* 14: And we lærað þæt preosta gehwilc tilige him rihtlice, and ne beo ænig mangere[2] mid unrihte ne gitsigende massere.

---

[1] Jost, 'Einige Wulfstantexte', p. 296.
[2] X14 *man geara* is obviously wrong.

To this example of Jost's, convincing because of his stylistic argument, may be added a further one in which there appears to be no question of any other source:

> Ælfric I, 85: Se preost sceal habban gehalgodne ele on sundron to cildum *and* on sundran to seocum mannu*m*.
>
> *Can.* 69: And we læraðþæt preosta gehwilc ægðer hæbbe ge fulluhtele ge seocum smyrels.

Equally definite cases of borrowing can be cited to prove that Wulfstan used both of the OE. letters written for him, Ælfric II and III:

> Ælfric II, 161–2: Beo his calic geworht of ecum antimbre, gylden oþþe sylfren, glæsen oþþe tinen.
> Ne beo he na hyrnen ne huru treowen.
>
> *Can.* 41: And we læraðþæt ælc calic gegoten beo þe man husl on halgige, and on treowenum ne halgige man ænig.

Although this requirement is to be found also in I, 58 and 2, 141, we are justified in regarding II, 161–2 as the source, as it alone shares with *Canons* 41 the explicit ban on a wooden chalice.

> Ælfric III, 80: And ic secge eow to soþan, *þæt* ge sceolan læran cnapan *and* geonge men eow to fultume, *þæt* hig æfter eow don þa ylcan þenunga.
>
> *Can.* 51: And we læraðþæt preostas geoguðe geornlice læran, and to cræftan teon, þæt hi ciricfultum habban.

Here the parallel is closer than that afforded by Ælfric 3, 40 or Theodulf's *Capitula* XX.

It cannot be proved that Ælfric 3, the *Second Latin Letter for Wulfstan*, was laid under contribution in the writing of the *Canons*. But although none of its articles can be described as an immediate source, there are one or two passages which duplicate ideas which Wulfstan took from other sources. For example, 3, 25 approximates to I, 107, which is almost certainly the source of *Canons* 28, and 3, 68 and 71 say the same as *Canons* 40, but are no closer to it than 2a, XI–XII or III, 93–4 and 97. On the other hand, it is certain that Wulfstan used the Latin Ælfric 2 in three of the canons: 8, 31, and 15. No source other than 2, 163 can be found for the requirement in *Can.* X15[1] that a child should be baptised within seven days. The parallel passages are set out in the Commentary.

[1] There is no evidence to support the *xxxvii nihtum* of D, and in these circumstances the version in X must be preferred. Thirty-seven days is an

INTRODUCTION   xli

Excerptiones pseudo-Ecgberti[1]

The relation between this text and the *Canons* is by no means as doubtful as is implied by Professor Bethurum.[2] From Ælfric's considerable use of these *Excerptiones*, and the inclusion in the *Canons* of material from Ælfric which is derived from this source, it might appear that Wulfstan knew the *Excerptiones* only by way of Ælfric. Direct indebtedness can, however, be demonstrated in a number of instances, the most striking of which is *Canons* 39:

> And we læraðˈ þæt næfre preost ne geþristlæce þæt he mæssige buton he eal hæbbe þæt to husle gebirige: þæt is clæne oflete, and clæne win, and clæne wæter. Wa ðam þe mæssian onginð buton he ælc þara habbe, and wa ðam þe þar ful þing todeð þonne gelice þam þe Iudeas didon þa hi mængdon eced and geallan togædere and hit siððan on bismer Criste gebudon.
>
> *Exc. pseudo-Ecgberti* C: Sacerdotes Dei diligenter semper procurent, ut panis et vinum, et aqua, sine quibus nequaquam missae celebrantur, pura et munda fiant; quia si aliter agatur, cum his qui acetum cum felle mixtum Domino optulerunt . . . punientur.

Other clear cases of borrowing are *Canons* 20, part of 45, 46, 47, 54, 55, and 56. Of these, the verbal resemblance which gives the first sign of the borrowing is confirmed by secondary evidence in 46, 47, and 54, 55, 56. *Canons* 46 appears to come from *Exc. pseudo-Ecgberti* CLIV; this suspicion is confirmed by the fact that 47 is a clear instance of borrowing from the immediately preceding section of the *Excerptiones*, CLIII. The position is the same with regard to 54–5 and 56. Professor Bethurum viewed the additional section in X, which requires a tripartite division of alms, as crucial in determining the relationship of the *Canons* to the *Excerptiones*, and that of the two versions of the *Canons*.[3] In fact, the present examination of the sources shows that the difficulty can be cleared up quite easily. Professor Bethurum must have been unaware, at the time she wrote her article, of the general indebtedness of the *Canons* to the *Excerptiones*, regarding X56 (part of 55 in Thorpe, the only text available at the time) as a possibly spurious addition.

unreasonably long period, as the whole point of this article is to ensure that children should be baptized as soon after birth as possible. See Commentary under *Can.* 15.

[1] A heterogeneous collection of Frankish decrees. Fehr gives its sources on pp. xcvii–xcix of *Die Hirtenbriefe Ælfrics*.
[2] 'Archbishop Wulfstan's Commònplace Book', *P.M.L.A.* lvii (1942), 919.
[3] Ibid.

However, it seems that X56 is derived from *Exc. pseudo-Ecgberti* V, and now that it appears that the debt to the *Excerptiones* is considerable, the authenticity of this section can hardly be doubted. But the issue is complicated by the fact that Ælfric I, 68 reproduces *Excerptiones* V very faithfully, and thus claims equal consideration as an immediate source. On examining the neighbouring articles of the *Canons*, however, one finds that 54 is derived from *Excerptiones* IV, and that 55 may well have been suggested by the beginning of *Excerptiones* V. This, in my opinion, proves that Wulfstan had *Excerptiones* V rather than Ælfric I, 68 in mind when he wrote *Canons* 56, that this extra section is genuine, and that we are faced with a case of simple omission from D.[1]

The penitential of pseudo-Theodore

The influence of the penitential falsely attributed to Theodore can be seen in *Canons* 16, 18, 19, 38, and perhaps 53. Although the influence of *pseudo-Theodore* on *Canons* 16, the section dealing with heathen practices, is obvious, the presence of other source-material makes the borrowing too complex to be presented here. *Canons* 19: *pseudo-Theodore* XXXVIII, 8 gives a clearer example:

> And we lærað þæt man geswice sunnandæges cypinge and folcgemota. Opera vero servilia diebus Dominicis nullo modo agantur; id est . . . nec ad placita conveniant.

De Regula Canonicorum (Homily Xa)

This is an OE. translation, proved by Jost to have been made by Wulfstan, of a chapter of Amalarius of Metz's *De Regula Canonicorum*.[2] The influence of this translation can be seen in, for example, *Canons* 13, and less directly in other sections which reflect Homily Xc, which is itself derived from Xa.

> *Can.* 13: And we lærað þæt ænig forðboren preost ne forseo þone læsborenan . . . .
> Xa, 46–7: . . . ne ða æþelborenan ne lean þa læsborenan.

The penitential of pseudo-Ecgbert

This OE. translation of a penitential by Halitgar of Cambrai was a popular source in the late AS. period. Passages of the *Canons*

---

[1] See parallels quoted in Commentary to *Can.* 54–6.
[2] 'Einige Wulfstantexte', pp. 267–8.

which are derived from it are 21, part of 65, 66, and part of X16:

Can. X16: ... ðone deofles cræft þe man dryhð þær man þa cild þurh þa eorðan tihð.
Pen. pseudo-Ecgbert IV, 16: Wif⟨man⟩ beo þæs ylcan wyrðe, gif heo tilað hire cilde mid ænigum wiccecræft oððe æt wega gelætan purh [*sic*] ⟨þa⟩ eorðan tyhð.

The Homilia *of Pope Leo IV*

Jost quotes some phrases from this work in connection with *Canons* 33 and 42.[1] The resemblance is quite close, and they deserve to be considered as sources:

Can. 33: And we lærað þæt ælc preost habbe corporalem þonne he mæssige and subumlem (X subumbrale) under his alban, and eal mæssereaf wurðlice behworfen.
Homilia: Nullus cantet ... sine amictu, sine alba ... vestimenta nitida sint ... Corporale mundissimum sit.

There is a parallel to this in Ælfric I, 55, but this has no mention of specific vestments, and the parallel *mæssereaf wurðlice behworfen*: *vestimenta nitida sint* is not found.

Can. 42: ... and a sy byrnende leoht on circan þonne man mæssan singe.
Homilia: Nullus cantet sine lumine.

This requirement is not stated so directly anywhere else in the authorities habitually used by Wulfstan. Ælfric I, 33 and II, 104 imply the use of a light at Mass, but do so merely incidentally while defining the duties of an acolyte.

On this evidence alone it would be reasonable to claim the *Homilia* as a source for these two articles. In fact, the contribution of this little-known work appears to be greater than this. In the Commentary parallels from the *Homilia* are cited for *Canons* 8, 9, 25, 30, 33, 35, 36, 40, 42, 44, and 58. In all cases except 33 and 42, Ælfric or Theodulf can be quoted as the immediate source. It will be noticed that, apart from 25 and 58, only two topics are involved —respect for one's fellow priests in 8 and 9, and the conduct of the Mass in the other seven; moreover, these seven sections on the Mass are concentrated in one group of adjacent sections of the *Canons*.

[1] *Polity*, pp. 190, 194.

The *Homilia* is, although short, something of a specialist work on the Mass. It is largely dependent on Theodulf (who died in 821, and so was a near-contemporary of Leo) but on this one topic it goes into rather fuller detail. It was possibly the influence of this work which led Wulfstan to write what is virtually a separate section on the priest's conduct at Mass. Neither Ælfric nor Theodulf, who provide immediate sources if we are to judge by similarities of wording, has the concentration on this subject which the *Homilia* and the *Canons of Edgar* both have: a group of early chapters of the *Capitula* discusses the Mass, but in less detail than either of these works; and the immediate source-material in Ælfric is scattered throughout the *Pastoral Letters*. Most significant, Wulfstan preserves the sequence of the *Homilia* in the first half of his section on the Mass. The extracts below follow the order of phrases in the *Homilia*:

Can. 35: And we lærað þæt ænig mæssepreost ana ne mæssige . . .
Hom.: Nullus missam cantet solus . . .

Can. 36: And we lærað þæt ænig unfæstende man husles ne abirige . . .
Hom.: . . . nullus cantet eam nisi jejunus . . .

Can. 40: And we læraþ þæt æfre ne gewurðe þæt preost mæssige and silf þæt husl ne geþicge . . .
Hom.: Nullus cantet qui non communicet . . .

Can. 42: And a sy byrnende leoht on circan þonne man mæssan singe.
Hom.: Nullus cantet sine lumine . . .

After this the sequence is disturbed, a continuous passage in the *Homilia* appearing as *Canons* 33 (part), 44 (?), 33 (part), 30. But although the order of ideas is broken, the concentration on a single set of ideas which characterizes the *Homilia* is preserved in the compact central section of the *Canons*.

If we accept these parallels as evidence of borrowing, the relationship between the two works is not difficult to explain. Contrary to his usual practice, by which he rearranged the contents of his sources very considerably, Wulfstan to some extent adopted the layout of his source in this particular case, because it was a concise though comprehensive work which gave most of his material for the central section of his *Canons*. The style, however, is most unsuitable for his purpose—excessively terse and elliptical, quite unlike Wulfstan's style. For this reason he read Ælfric, and on the surface it is the influence of this writer rather than of Leo IV which appears.

But if we consider Leo as a source, there is still one difficulty which the hypothesis of the last paragraph—a hypothesis not unlike many which are necessary to hold the Wulfstan canon together— cannot resolve. All the other source-texts are found in Wulfstan's 'commonplace-book' manuscripts, and, as will be seen in the next part of the Introduction, this fact is important to the interpretation and evaluation of the *Canons of Edgar*. The *Homilia* does not occur in the 'commonplace-book' manuscripts; nor is there any evidence that it ever did, or that it was ever in a manuscript which Wulfstan might have known. There is, then, no external evidence that Wulfstan knew the *Homilia*, although there is external evidence for his knowledge of the 'commonplace-book' sources. In spite of this, we can argue that the *Homilia* is a source, as the internal evidence in favour of this assumption is of exactly the same order as that used in proving Ælfric's contribution, or Theodulf's. In view of these facts, it is postulated that the relationship between the *Homilia* and the *Canons* is of a different kind from that between the 'commonplace-book' sources and the *Canons*: that the *Homilia* came into Wulfstan's hands separately, and in a manner which cannot now be explained; and that this separateness is reflected in the separateness of the *Homilia*-derived material in the *Canons*, as opposed to the thorough intermingling of the 'commonplace-book' material.[1]

IV. THE RELATIONSHIP OF THE CANONS OF EDGAR TO WULFSTAN'S OTHER WORKS

There has been very little fruitful discussion of the *Canons of Edgar* as a historical document; nor have its place and purpose in the framework of Wulfstan's complete works been adequately studied. Several nineteenth-century historians refer to Thorpe's *Canons Enacted under King Edgar*, but useful criticism was impossible until Jost had separated the real *Canons* from the penitential texts printed with it by Thorpe, and had demonstrated Wulfstan's authorship.[2] Discussion earlier than Jost's article was

---

[1] For a further note on the *Homilia*, see p. lxi below.
[2] K. Jost, 'Einige Wulfstantexte', pp. 288–301. This remains the only detailed study of the *Canons*.

necessarily confusing at best and ill founded at worst.[1] Two of Ure's references to the *Canons*, which he identifies by the page numbers of the whole of Thorpe's *Canons enacted under King Edgar*, and which he states contain *De Confessione* (one of the penitential texts), show that the confusion still exists.[2]

Does a relatively short text like this merit intensive study? This question is partly answered by the number of scattered references to it which can be found in works on Wulfstan published during the last thirty years: in, for example, Professor Bethurum's edition of the Homilies and her article 'Archbishop Wulfstan's Commonplace Book'.[3] The points of correspondence between the *Canons of Edgar* and the Homilies and Laws are much more numerous than these references and those in my own Commentary suggest. Like the *Institutes of Polity*, the *Canons* may be important in establishing a consistent purpose in Wulfstan's work: to effect certain far-reaching reforms by practical legislation (in the non-homiletic works) and by passionate exhortation. I subscribe to Professor Whitelock's picture of Wulfstan as an ardent reformer and 'a man well versed in canonistic literature, excerpting carefully from Latin authors before writing his vernacular sermons . . .'.[4] This picture can be made much clearer by close study of the *Canons of Edgar*, which was central in Wulfstan's programme of reform; it also demonstrates better than any other of his works the deliberateness with which he familiarized himself with the best canonical writings to provide a basis of accepted authority for his reforms.

Wulfstan's programme of reforms was a wide-ranging one, aimed at all orders of society. Its scope is indicated by the range of subject-matter in the *Institutes of Polity*.[5] Both versions of this work begin by stating the responsibilities of a Christian king; then the conventional division is made of Oratores, Laboratores, and Bellatores; a brief summary of the functions of each group follows, and then Wulfstan deals in turn with the duties and responsibilities of specific classes of society: bishops, ðeodwitan, earls, reeves, secular priests, regular clergy (abbots, monks, nuns), laity, widows, and finally two sections *Be eallum cristenum mannum*. The wide

---

[1] I refer particularly to mentions of the 'so-called *Canons of Edgar*' by Selborne, Stubbs, Oakley, and McNeill and Gamer.
[2] *The Benedictine Office* (Edinburgh, 1957), pp. 29, 51–2.
[3] *P.M.L.A.* lvii (1942), 916–29.
[4] *T.R.H.S.* 4th series, xxiv (1942), 30.
[5] Edited by K. Jost, Bern, 1959.

range is paralleled in the Homilies, and is consistent with Wulfstan's position as archbishop and as the most influential English statesman of his time.

The picture of nation-wide degeneracy painted in the *Sermo Lupi* implies a need for an over-all scheme of reform. This need is met by the legal codes written up by Wulfstan, which culminate in II Cnut, the latest and most comprehensive of them.[1] This, like *Polity*, is directed at all ranks of society, civil and ecclesiastical. Outside the laws, Wulfstan's writings treat of more specific sections of society: laity, bishops, regular clergy, and above all secular clergy. His concern for the conduct of the secular clergy is easy to explain. First, they had received less attention than the regular clergy in the Church reforms since Edgar's time: their status and duties were not so well defined. Second, they were Wulfstan's most important subordinates in the administration of his dioceses. Third, Wulfstan, as Archbishop of York, must have been concerned because earlier reform had scarcely touched the northern province. Fourth, and perhaps most important, Wulfstan viewed lay morality and welfare as the responsibility of the clergy as much as of individual laymen. Lay reform was to be accomplished by preaching and practical instruction by the clergy, and by their assiduous care over the spiritual needs of the congregation. The *Canons of Edgar* is a kind of *Pastoral Letter* addressed to the secular clergy, outlining their status, their standards of morality, and their responsibilities towards their flocks.

Wulfstan's zeal for reform and his concern for the secular clergy are consistent with what we know of the history of ecclesiastical reform from Edgar onwards. In the late eighth and ninth centuries the monastic foundations of England had, like those of the Continent, ignored the strictness of the Rule and become increasingly secularized:

... in north and south alike, the tendency, common in every country and century of the early Middle Ages, for the monastic life to lose its regular character, and for houses to become merely clerical establishments or to fall wholly under lay control, was making itself felt more and more strongly.[2]

[1] The argument for Wulfstan's authorship is given by Professor Whitelock in *E.H.R.* lxiii (1948), 433–52.
[2] Dom David Knowles, *The Monastic Order in England* (Oxford, 1949), p. 23. My brief summary is based on chapters i–iv of his account.

It seems that we can accept at its face value Alfred's gloomy picture of the state of monastic culture at the end of the ninth century. When he decided to establish a monastery at Athelney, he was forced to bring clerics from the Continent to govern it, and even had to import novices to populate it. He founded a nunnery at Shaftesbury.

Alfred's monastic reforms had little permanent effect: the community at Athelney certainly did not flourish, and that at Winchester was occupied by secular priests by the time of Edgar's reforms, and may indeed never have been regular. When Edgar came to the throne of Wessex in 959, he was faced with a situation almost as bad as that which had confronted Alfred. But his own energy, and the efforts of Æthelwold, Oswald, and especially Dunstan, enabled him to effect a complete reform.[1] Before Dunstan was consecrated Bishop of Worcester,[2] he had been active in the reform of Glastonbury, which was probably a house of secular clerks. Æthelwold had been sent to Abingdon in 954 for the reform of that house; in 964, as Bishop of Winchester, he expelled the secular clergy from the Old Minster and replaced them by regular monks from Abingdon, and in the next year removed the secular clerks from King Edward's New Minster. From this time on Edgar's three bishops concerned themselves in the establishment, refounding, or reform of over thirty regular houses.[3] As a result of the efforts of these reforming bishops, the monastic houses reached what Dom Knowles describes as 'a kind of apogee' in the last five years of Edgar's reign. The last twenty years of the century saw a consolidation of the position established by Edgar's reformers; the monasteries became prosperous and were recognized as centres of learning and culture.[4]

If we accept Knowles's view of this period, it is clear that Wulfstan had no need to exhort the monks to morality, as his penitential sources had done, nor to learning, as Alfred had. Only two of his works are addressed to the regular clergy: Homily Xa (*De Regula Canonicorum*), and certain sections of *Polity*. *De Regula Canonicorum* is a straightforward set of rules for communal life. Its brevity

---

[1] Knowles, op. cit., pp. 36–56.

[2] By Edgar as King of Mercia in 957. The reform of Glastonbury dates from 943 or 944.

[3] Knowles, p. 52. Only about six houses were reformed between the time of Dunstan and the Conquest.

[4] See Knowles, pp. 58–61 for a description of the state of affairs in monastic houses in the period immediately before Wulfstan's episcopacy.

and lack of condemnation imply that Wulfstan was not very anxious about regular clerks. However, I *Polity* 78–86 (= II *Polity* 170–86) make it clear that the monastic clergy are not forgotten, and VIII Atr. 31–31, I give them a serious warning:

> Ac we lærað georne 7 luflice biddað, þæt ælces hades m*en* þ*am* life libban, þe heo*m* to gebirige.
> 7 heonan forð we willað, þæt abbodas 7 munecas regollicor libban, þonn*e* hi nu ær ðisan on gewunan hæfdon.

The *Canons of Edgar* largely[1] ignores the regular clergy, perhaps because the relatively independent way of life of monks minimized their influence on the morality of the country as a whole. We must look more closely into the whole movement of ecclesiastical reform to discover the cause of Wulfstan's concern for the conduct of the secular clergy. R. R. Darlington has pointed out that concentration on monastic reforms has tended to obscure the fact

> that the reformers were aiming at something more than a revival of strict monastic observances. They were endeavouring, partly by personal influence and partly through the medium of their cathedral churches, which became centres of learning, to rouse the enthusiasm of the secular clergy.[2]

Darlington goes on to show how the bishops of the early eleventh century carried on this tradition: many of them were educated in houses reformed during Edgar's reign, and so naturally continued in the spirit of Dunstan and his contemporaries. We cannot be certain about Wulfstan's early career, but at the height of his power he was exactly the type of reforming prelate whom Darlington describes: the above quotation is as accurate a description of Wulfstan as of the men of Dunstan's more immediate circle and following.

Darlington includes Wulfstan, whom he calls 'an ardent reformer', in the number of late Anglo-Saxon bishops who were firmly in the reforming tradition of Dunstan, Æthelwold, and Oswald.[3] Professor Whitelock summarizes his multifarious

---

[1] Except for the mention of *mynsterpreost* in *Can.* D46; but see Commentary.

[2] R. R. Darlington, 'Ecclesiastical Reform in the late OE. Period', *E.H.R.* li (1936), 387–8. He illustrates this statement by giving details of the wider, non-monastic reforming activities of Oswald and Dunstan.

[3] Darlington, p. 392: [Wulfsige and Wulfstan] 'were ardent reformers who aimed at raising the standards of the secular clergy'. He does not connect the *Canons* with Wulfstan.

reforming activities with more particular reference to his writings, and so elaborates and makes more specific Darlington's comments:

> ... Wulfstan was evidently active in religious reform by his own studies, by encouragement of manuscript compilation, by the issue of a rule of life for Canons and a code for the priesthood in general, by the circulation of pastoral letters for the clergy of his diocese and by the preaching of homilies to the laity ...[1]

As an energetic archbishop and bishop, Wulfstan must have been concerned with the administration of the smaller units in his dioceses. The secular priests, unlike the 'reformed' regular clergy, must have enjoyed unprecedented responsibility and opportunity for freedom. They suffered from lack of direction from the Church, and, it would appear, those who were put in charge of individual churches took advantage of their opportunity to re-establish the life of ease to which they had been traditionally accustomed in the communal houses. Wulfstan preached against neglectful priests in the homily printed as XVIb by Professor Bethurum:

> And wa þam hirdum ... þe estað heom silfum swa heom betst licað 7 godcundre heorde ne gimeð to nahte. (ll. 11–13)

The *Canons of Edgar* is a document designed to combat the immorality and laziness of the secular clergy and to give them practical guidance on the carrying out of their duties. There is no doubt that it is directed specifically to the secular clergy: *Canons* 8 is addressed to the priest who is ordained to a particular church, and *Canons* 6 refers to his *scriftscir*. The duties which are prescribed—baptism, celebration of Mass, administering penance and extreme unction—are those of the parochial priest with a lay congregation. The work would seem to be a kind of pastoral letter intended for general circulation: Wulfstan may have got the idea from Ælfric's *Pastoral Letters*, to which he was heavily indebted for material. His requests to Ælfric for information on both practical and theological matters make sense when we see him as earnestly engaged in compiling a work fuller of practical detail than any he had yet written.

The sections on morality and general conduct reflect a programme both of reform and growth. *Canons* 1–14 stress the need for

---

[1] 'Archbishop Wulfstan, Homilist and Statesman', *T.R.H.S.* (4th series), xxiv (1942), 35.

the stability of secular clergy: each priest is to stay with the church to which he was ordained for the whole of his life (8); he is to respect his fellow priests (2, 12–13), and not interfere in their affairs (9, 10); disputes are to be settled by the bishop (7); the importance of the synod for settling disputes and receiving guidance is pointed out (3–6). For the future, boys are to be trained for the ministry, to help priests in their old age and to carry on good traditions (51; cf. 10 and 12). This is reminiscent of Alfred's educational programme (as are Wulfstan's efforts in the field of manuscript compilation). The sections on general matters of clerical conduct are supplemented by specific directions on morality (58–66). These forbid major sins like lechery, drunkenness, and gaming, and are there partly, as we have seen, because the secular priests were less 'reformed' than the regular, and perhaps partly because of the strictness of Wulfstan's penitential sources.

The greater part of the *Canons* consists of detailed directions on the duties of the clergy. These directions divide into two categories: details of church practices which must be carried out by the priest, and lay activities which the priest must regulate by preaching.

The first duty which is dealt with after the general introduction is baptism (15). Wulfstan must have seen baptism as the greatest defence against paganism—perhaps it is significant that the section which follows (16) consists of a violent condemnation of heathen practices. Like Ælfric, Wulfstan stressed the need for the early baptism of infants in case they should die while still 'pagans'.[1] The importance of baptism was so great for him that he wrote a long *Sermo de Baptismate* (Homily VIIIc), an interpretation of the ritual of baptism and an exhortation to fulfil the promises.[2]

Sections 26–9 inform the priest that he must pay the greatest reverence to his church, and do his utmost to prevent its being used for secular purposes. The use of deserted churches as storehouses or cattle-sheds in the Middle Ages is well known, and is condemned by Ælfric.[3] Here it seems that Wulfstan is aiming at the reform of a specific and prevalent abuse.

Canons 30–44 constitute a homogeneous section on the conduct of the Mass. This is the most detailed part of the whole work, and

[1] Ælfric 2, 63: *ut non sint pagani ultra septem dies.*
[2] Cf. *Homilies*, pp. 302–4 and Commentary below under *Can.* 22.
[3] Ælfric III, 115.

aims at settling disputed points once for all. Wulfstan prescribes the necessary equipment for the celebration of Mass: the priest's vestments, the book, the taper, even the materials of which a chalice may be made. Procedure is carefully indicated, and there is some insistence on the cleanliness of ingredients and utensils. None of this is new: as Professor Bethurum pointed out, 'As a liturgist Wulfstan made no conspicuous contributions... (he) was content to leave much of the detail to Ælfric.'[1] In this section Wulfstan has assembled material from the most authoritative sources, in order to give guidance to his priests on every detailed point which might be disputed or which might give rise to laxity.

Canons 52 is an important section:

> And we lærað þæt preostas ælce sunnandæge folce bodigan and aa wel bisnian.

Wulfstan stressed the necessity of preaching to the laity at several points in his works, frequently enough for Professor Bethurum to refer to 'Wulfstan's favourite subject, the duty of priests to preach to and admonish the people'.[2] This is, in Wulfstan's eyes, one of the prime duties of the clergy; by preaching to the laity they can achieve the Archbishop's plan of the reform of the laity. The first of the sections of *Polity* on secular priests opens by saying that the priest's main task is to lead and preach to the people:

> Riht is, þæt sacerdas on heora scriftscirum willice *and* wærlice læran *and* lædan þa godcundan heorda, þe hig healdan sculon.
> And ægðer hi sculon, ge wel bodian ge wel bisnian *and* Godes circan geornlice lufian *and* for eal cristen folc geornlice gebiddan.[3]

Because the morality of laymen is the priest's concern, many parts of the *Canons* list sins which the laity must avoid, and duties they must observe. *Canons* 16 forbids paganism; 17 and 22 require the learning of the Pater Noster and Creed; 18, 19, 23–5 deal with the observance of feast- and fast-days; 20 and 21 forbid foolish behaviour and adultery respectively; 53 forbids the drinking of blood; 54–7 exhort the laity to render alms and tithes conscientiously.[4]

---

[1] *Homilies*, p. 83.   [2] *Homilies*, p. 348.
[3] I *Polity* 66–7 (= II *Polity* 102–3).
[4] Note that the late codes of Ethelred and Cnut's two codes draw extensively on these sections on the morality of laymen; this is a measure of the importance both of these particular sections and of the *Canons* in general. Cf. the derived *Northumbrian Priests' Law* as another indication of the importance of the

In summary, the *Canons of Edgar* is designed to control the morality of the secular clergy and to provide guidance on their duties. These duties are seen as responsibilities towards the laity: the priest must minister to his flock and exhort them to virtue. In the *Canons* we find the key to much of Wulfstan's programme of reform. The secular priest is one of the crucial figures in the reform of the nation; but in recent reforms he has received less guidance than any other cleric. He is important because he has the greatest opportunity for moral guidance of the bulk of the population. The *Canons of Edgar* tells him in what ways he must reform himself; exactly how he must perform his spiritual functions; and what areas of lay behaviour are most in need of regulation. The *Canons of Edgar* is thus aimed at the reform of the laity through the reform of the previously neglected and neglectful secular clergy; it provides a practical way of avoiding the catastrophe which Wulfstan describes in a moving passage from *Polity*:

> Hwæt gefaraðponne æt Godes egeslican dome þa hyrdas, þe ne cunnan [gehealdan] þa godcundan heorda, þe Crist mid his agenum life gebohte, *and* þe hy healdan scoldan, gif hy cuþan?
>
> Ac [hy] naþor þurh larlæste hy ne cunnan ne lædan, **ne læran**, ne lacnian hy rihtlice.
>
> Mid hwam wene we, forgyldað hy hy þonne?
>
> Wa heom, *þæt* hy æfre underfengan, *þæt* hy gehealdan ne cuþan!
>
> La, hu mæg blind man oþerne lædan? Hu mæg unlæred þe ma oðerne læran? . . .
>
> . . . 'Wa þam sacerdum', he cwæð, 'þe fretað and forswelgað folces synna.'
>
> *þæt* syndan þa, þe nellaþ oþþon ne cunnan oþþon ne durran **folc wið** synna gewarnian *and* synna gestyran, ac gyrnað þeh heora sceatta on teoþungum *and* on eallum cyricgerihtum,
>
> *and* naþor ne hy mid bysnungum wel ne lædaþ, ne mid bodungum wel ne læraðne, ne mid dædbotum wel ne lacniaþ, ne mid gebedrædenne fore ne þingiað, . . .[1]

Because the *Canons of Edgar* was intended to play such an important part in Wulfstan's scheme of reform, he took care that it

---

Canons. This text is edited by Liebermann (*Gesetze* I, 380–5) and translated by Professor Whitelock in *English Historical Documents*, i. 434–9, with an introductory note connecting it with Wulfstan.

[1] II *Polity* 114–18, 122–4.

should be doctrinally correct and backed by accepted authority. To this end he consulted a wide range of sources, both English and continental. His research into authorities was probably greater for the *Canons* than for any earlier work. We know also that he wrote to Ælfric for advice on various doctrinal matters, and that he encouraged his secretaries to make manuscript collections of canonistic writings.[1] Neither of these facts has yet been connected with the *Canons of Edgar*. The writing to Ælfric is a minor point: Wulfstan's original request is lost, and his borrowing from the *Private Letter to Wulfstan* is slight compared with his borrowing from the five *Pastoral Letters*. It is tempting to suppose that Wulfstan's intention to compile the *Canons* was his reason for writing to Ælfric for information, but this is probably unimportant and in any case unprovable.

What is provable is that there is a definite link between Wulfstan's assembling of sources for the *Canons of Edgar* and those later Wulfstan manuscripts which resemble one another in containing more or less the same collection of canonistic and penitential works: the so-called 'commonplace-book' manuscripts. The purpose of such a collection becomes clear when we see it in use in *one* work of Wulfstan's.[2] There is even a case for arguing that Wulfstan made the collection with the *Canons* in mind.

In 1895 Miss Mary Bateson, discussing the contents of MS. C.C.C.C. 265, suggested that it appeared to represent a bishop's reference-book:

The purpose of the writer in copying out a quantity of extracts, taken from various sources, seems to have been to make a kind of theological commonplace-book specially intended for a bishop's use.[3]

She notes that several other manuscripts appear to have a similar function, and specifies C.C.C.C. 190, Cotton Nero A. 1, Bodleian 718, and Bibl. Nat., Paris, Fonds Latin 3182, 'to name only those which do not merely resemble C.C.C.C. 265 in general character, but are also closely similar in detail. In these manuscripts the same extracts show a tendency to recur in the same or closely similar

---

[1] See D. Bethurum, 'Archbishop Wulfstan's Commonplace Book', *P.M.L.A.* lvii (1942); D. Whitelock, *T.R.H.S.* xxiv (1942).

[2] For the following discussion, see my ' "Archbishop Wulfstan's Commonplace-book" and the *Canons of Edgar*', *Medium Ævum*, xxxii (1963), 1–10.

[3] 'A Worcester Cathedral Book of Ecclesiastical Collections, Made *c*. 1000 A.D.', *E.H.R.* x (1895), 712.

INTRODUCTION

sequence...' (p. 712). Then she proceeds to list in some detail the contents of C.C.C.C. 265, noting the occurrence elsewhere of certain of the extracts. Her examination is an attempt to answer the question: 'Who collected these manuscripts? Where were they collected? What relation existed between the schools of learning in which the collections were made?' (p. 713).

Miss Bateson was unable to answer these questions in 1895, because of the immature state of development of Wulfstan studies at that date. But although she had no detailed information on Wulfstan, her description of the purpose of the manuscripts is substantially accurate. There can be no doubt that the contents alone of these manuscripts merit their being described as examples of a bishop's collection of key writings—a source-book or at least a reference-book: this much is certain without any external evidence.

Since 1895 studies of the manuscripts in question, and of Wulfstan, have made it possible to be more exact in answering Miss Bateson's questions. The complete list of manuscripts which must now be discussed with reference to the commonplace-book theory is as follows:

C.C.C.C. 190
C.C.C.C. 265
Bodley 718
Junius 121
Bibl. Nat., Paris, Fonds Latin 3182
Brussels, Bibliothèque Royale, 8558–63 (2498) (Bx)
Vespasian A. 14
Barlow 37
Copenhagen MS. Gl. Kgl. S. 1595.[1, 2]

In addition to the studies of these manuscripts listed below, three interpretative articles are of importance: those by Bethurum and Whitelock published in 1942, and B. Fehr, 'Das Benediktiner-Offizium und die Beziehungen zwischen Ælfric und Wulfstan', *Eng. Stud.* xlvi (1913), 337–46.[3]

---

[1] Studies of these manuscripts include: *Gesetze* I, xx f.; M. R. James, *A Descriptive Catalogue of the Manuscripts in the Library of Corpus Christi College, Cambridge*; B. Fehr, *Die Hirtenbriefe Ælfrics*, Bibl. der ang. Prosa, IX, x–xxii; J. Raith, *Bibl. der. ang. Prosa*, XIII, x–xiii; Ker, *Catalogue*.

[2] C.C.C.C. 201, pp. 179–272 (Ker, no. 50), containing both the OE. and Latin *Capitula*, might be added to the list.

[3] But see P. Clemoes, 'The Old English Benedictine Office, C.C.C.C. 190, and the relations between Ælfric and Wulfstan: a reconsideration', *Anglia*, lxxviii (1960), 265–83.

Fehr believed that the collection in C.C.C.C. 190 was compiled by Ælfric for Wulfstan, who later had it incorporated in C.C.C.C. 265. Ælfric was clearly the more learned of the two, at least initially, and we know that he provided Wulfstan with source material which was used in the archbishop's own writings. The major works in the set of manuscripts were the sources for Ælfric's *Pastoral Letters* as well as for Wulfstan.

Professor Bethurum's article states the case for Wulfstan's organization of the collection extremely clearly. She gives a summary of the external evidence for Wulfstan's connection with some of the manuscripts.[1] Then she shows how each of the major works occurring in several of the manuscripts is used more than once by Wulfstan (pp. 917–20), and finally demonstrates his indebtedness to various short extracts scattered throughout the manuscripts (pp. 920–4). She considers Wulfstan's use of these short passages even more significant than his borrowing from the larger works, because it is only when they are seen as his source material that their distribution in the manuscripts has any purpose or unity. Her conclusion is that Fehr may be right in suggesting that Ælfric supplied at least the basic material for Wulfstan's collection:

There is no doubt that the Abbot of Eynsham contributed a great deal to the training of his superior, and MS. 190 may well offer further evidence of his tutoring [pp. 927–8].

But Professor Bethurum gives Wulfstan the credit for assembling the collection in the form in which we know it:

The assembling of all the material in these MSS. . . . shows how Wulfstan worked to provide himself the necessary guides for his multifarious duties as archbishop [p. 929].

Her final statement is tentative:

A careful study of the sources of the *Canons of Edgar* and the *Institutes of Polity* will almost certainly reveal more evidence on how Wulfstan used a collection of this kind, and probably on the relation of these MSS. Until such a study is forthcoming, we may accept these parallels as some evidence of Wulfstan's hand in the ordering of the work [pp. 928–9].

---

[1] 'Archbishop Wulfstan's Commonplace Book', pp. 917, 929; in *Homilies* p. 99, n. 1, she corrects her earlier dating of C.C.C.C. 265, thus somewhat weakening its connection with Wulfstan.

INTRODUCTION

Professor Whitelock came to substantially the same conclusion as Professor Bethurum, in the same year and independently of her:

> ... taking into consideration what we know of Wulfstan's activity in excerpting passages from Latin authors ... it is surely more probable that the manuscript under discussion is based on a collection made at Worcester.[1]

The *Canons of Edgar* is perhaps the most widely eclectic of Wulfstan's works; there are very few of its sections which cannot be traced to one or other of a wide variety of sources. The value of a collection of sources such as that described by Professor Bethurum would be at its greatest for an author engaged in compiling a work as highly derivative as this. We could take a different viewpoint and say that the 'commonplace-book' as represented in C.C.C.C. 265 or 190 is clearly reflected in the range and ordering of the source material of the *Canons*.

What is most important is that the works used in the *Canons of Edgar* are exactly those which make up the chief contents of the manuscripts in question. The following are the most important sources of the *Canons*:

I Ælfric's *Pastoral Letters*
II Theodulf's *Capitula*
III *Excerptiones pseudo-Ecgberti*
IV *Penitential of pseudo-Theodore*
V *Penitential of pseudo-Ecgbert*
VI Amalarius of Metz's *De Regula Canonicorum*[2]

The distribution of these works in the manuscripts is indicated by the table on the following page, in which the roman numerals correspond with those in the list above.

The table overleaf shows the widespread distribution of these six works in the 'commonplace-book' manuscripts. As Miss Bateson

---

[1] Whitelock, op. cit., p. 34. For the whole discussion, which includes criticism of Fehr's view, see pp. 30–5.

[2] For comparison, Bethurum's list of the major works in the manuscripts (she considers their use in the *Canons* only incidentally) is as follows:

1. Theodulf's *Capitula*.
2. *Pen. pseudo-Theodore*.
3. *De Regula Canonicorum*.
4. Ælfric's *Pastoral Letters*.
5. Napier IV.
6. *Excerptiones pseudo-Ecgberti*.
7. *De Officiis Diurnalium siue Nocturnalium*.

pointed out, their recurrence in similar sequences argues that the manuscripts in which they occur have been copied from one single collection. The table suggests that C.C.C.C. 190 and 265 are nearest to the original collection, but it would be extremely difficult to establish the relationships between the other members of the group of manuscripts.

Whatever the details of the manuscripts' relationships may be, there is little doubt about the form and purpose of their prototype.

MS. source	I^1	II^2	III	IV	V	VI
CCCC 190	√		√	√	√	
CCCC 265	√	√	√	√		√
Bodley 718			√			
Junius 121	√				√	√
Nero A. I			√	√		
Fonds Latin 3182			√			
Barlow 37			√	√		
Copenhagen Gl. Kgl. S. 1595	√					√
Bx				√	√	

Professor Bethurum tentatively attributed the collection to the Worcester scriptorium as directed by Wulfstan, but had to rely for evidence on Wulfstan's use of very minor parts of the anthology: an argument which is hardly striking because it is so delicate. She was presumably unwilling to accept the evidence of the use of the larger works as conclusive because of their very probable availability separately, and because she had no example of their use together in a single work.[3]

The *Canons of Edgar* offers definite proof of Wulfstan's use of a collection of sources based mainly on the six works listed above. The *Canons* is very deeply indebted to most of the six, in terms of bulk of material alone. More important, the complexity with which the source material is intermingled suggests not just a hasty copying of key passages from the authorities, but a close study and

---

[1] The *Pastoral Letters* occur complete only in C.C.C.C. 190.

[2] The Latin and OE. versions of Theodulf's *Capitula* which occur in C.C.C.C. 201 were not, of course, originally a part of D; part of a different OE. translation occurs in Bodley 865.

[3] Cf. Bethurum, op. cit., p. 920.

comparison, leading to assimilation, which would be possible only if the sources were all readily accessible in collected form. Further, the influence of these six major sources can be seen throughout the *Canons*, while the *Homilia* of Leo, the only work not found in the commonplace-book manuscripts, is in the main restricted in its influence to the central section on the Mass.

The intermingling of passages from various sources can easily be studied in the Commentary. There are very few sections of the *Canons* for which two or three parallels cannot be found in the habitual sources, and very often a section betrays the influence of several writers in its wording as well as in its content. A fairly short and simple example is *Canons* 8, for which no less than seven parallels can be found:

> And we lærað þæt ænig preost silfwilles ne forlæte þa circan þe he to gebletsod wæs, ac hæbbe him þa to rihtæwe. (X adds: þa hwile þe his lif sig.)

Ælfric 2, 194–5:
> Non licet clerico dimittere ecclesiam suam, ad quam ordinatus est, et migrare ad alteram, sine permissu episcopi sui.
> Quia ecclesia est eius uxor spiritaliter, per quam spiritales filios generare debet.

Ælfric II, 207:
> Ne sceal nan preost his cyricean forlætan, þe he to ge-hadod bið *and* to oþere faran, buton his bisceop lyfe for sumon ge-sceade.

De Regula Canonicorum 12–13:
> ... ac healdan heora riht æwe, þæt is heora mynster.

I *Polity* 77 (= II *Polity* 153):
> Cirice is sacerdos æwe.

Ælfric I, 73:
> Ne nan preost ne fare for ænigre gitsunge fram mynstre to oðrum, ac æfre þurhwunige þær he to gehadod wæs, þa hwyle þe his dagas beoð.

Excerptiones pseudo-Ecgberti XIII:
> ... usque ad vitae ... exitum.

Leo, *Homilia* 679:
> Nullus ecclesiam, ad quam intitulatus est, dimittat, et ad aliam, quaestus gratia, sine licentia episcopi migret.

No further proof is necessary that Wulfstan was responsible for having the collection made, and that he made the fullest use of it in the *Canons*. Can we go further and show that he made the collection with the *Canons of Edgar* in mind? The date of the *Canons* would seem to indicate this. The *Canons* can be dated after Ælfric's *Pastoral Letters* and before V Atr., that is to say somewhere between 1005 and 1007. The collection of the 'commonplace-book' must have taken place before 1007, the *terminus ad quem* for the *Canons*. The *terminus a quo* is probably the same as that for the *Canons*, because the *Pastoral Letters* form the nucleus of the collection. It is not difficult to believe that Wulfstan had the idea for his *Canons of Edgar* from the *Pastoral Letters*; that in the two or three years before 1005-6 he prepared a collection of sources for his own letter to the clergy, based on the *Pastoral Letters*; that he wrote to Ælfric for information through the same motive.

A further reason for believing that Wulfstan collected the material in the 'commonplace-book' manuscripts in the years immediately preceding the writing of the *Canons of Edgar* is that none of the major sources of the *Canons*, i.e. none of the main contents of the manuscripts in question, is used extensively before the *Canons*.[1] Passages reminiscent of one or other of the six main sources start occurring in the homilies about the time when Wulfstan was writing what Professor Bethurum calls the 'Christian Life' group.[2] These homilies are more doctrinally factual and specific than those of the preceding group, the eschatological homilies written early in his career. We may recall Professor Bethurum's chronology for the homilies immediately preceding the *Canons*: Xa, VI, VII, IX, XI, VIIIa, VIIIb, Xb, Xc.[3] I suggest that about the beginning of this central period of his writing career Wulfstan's contact with Ælfric began to be productive. With a view to writing a serious and influential work for the secular clergy, Wulfstan began to make a collection of canonistic literature, starting with Ælfric's *Pastoral Letters*, and soon adding his own translation of *De Regula Canonicorum*. As the collection grew, it began more and more clearly to influence the homilies written at the same time: for example, VII is the first to show the influence of Theodulf's *Capitula*. Xc, written immediately before the *Canons*, depends more than any previous homily on the collection. Then came the

[1] Except Amalarius' *De Regula Canonicorum*, which is translated as Xa.
[2] Homilies VI–XII.
[3] *Homilies*, p. 103.

Canons of Edgar, the first work to be based wholly on it. Writings after the *Canons* are heavily indebted both to the collection and to the *Canons* itself; Homily VIIIc, *Polity*, and above all the legal codes.[1] The *Northumbrian Priests' Law* is a later rewriting of the *Canons*, intended for secular clergy in the northern diocese.

I consider that the evidence of the sources of the *Canons of Edgar*, added to that produced by Professor Bethurum, suggests that Archbishop Wulfstan made his commonplace-book with the writing of the *Canons* in mind. No other of his works is so thoroughly dependent on the sources contained in the collection, and no earlier work shows much knowledge of these sources. The collection must have been made in the two or three years preceding the *Canons*—its *termini* are in fact the same as those for the *Canons*. If my argument for the importance of the *Canons of Edgar* is accepted, then the intention to write this work was sufficient motive for the assembling of the collection.

ADDITIONAL NOTE

After the present edition had been completed and set up in print, three matters of interpretation and fact were brought to my attention by Professor Whitelock and Mr. N. R. Ker. It was not possible, unfortunately, to re-work my Introduction and Commentary extensively to accommodate these points at a late stage of printing, so I must content myself with simply noticing them here. First, Professor Whitelock has in recent years emphasized the claims of York as Wulfstan's centre of scholarship, arguing that Worcester was not his only centre, nor necessarily the more important of the two. Second, she has pointed out that Professor Clemoes's recent work on Ælfric may suggest some modification of my arguments about the date of the *Canons* and the contents of the 'commonplace-book'. Finally, Mr. Ker has informed me that the 'Homilia of Leo IV' is in fact part of an Ordo for a synod, and appears in a critical edition by Vogel and Elze, *Pontifical Romano-Germanique du dixième siècle*, Studi e Testi 226 (1963), 286–9. I have not been able to investigate further the status, date, and provenance of this text. Further study might necessitate some alteration to the conclusions of pp. xliii–xlv above.

---

[1] *Polity* is dated by Jost not earlier than 1008: '... so kann die I Polity kaum früher entstanden sein als 1008–10' (*Polity*, p. 33).

[...]pihtisþælc
[...]ƿa ƿal
[...]ode ꞽhuꞽnu pihte
[...]mæsepreost
[...]obþe þone þehī
[...]unfæstende man
[...]tꝼoꞃ oꝼeꞃ ꞅtoc
[...]ꞃeoꞃt aneꞃ dæꞹeꞅ
[...]þꞃiꞅa
[...]þꞃiþai mæꞅt ꞃa
[...]ꞹaꞃa huꞃel hæbbe
[...]nt onclænnyꞅꞅe
[...]ꝼoꞃ taloiꞹe ꞹyꝼ
[...]ꝼꞃeꞃu ꞅalaꞃu
[...]hiꞅ man bꞃucan
[...]e hit man onclænū
[...]ꝼꝏde ꞹebꞃinꞹe·
[...]hit ꝼoꞃ ꞹꝓnte·
[...]eꞃꞃiꞅtlæce· þhe ꝑꞅunꞇꜹꞇ·:
[...]ebbe· þ to huꞅte
[...]ltte· ꞏꞏꞏ ꞏ clæne pꞃn·
[...]æꞅꞃan onꞹinþ·

NOTE ON THE TEXT

THE texts from pp. 97–101 of D and ff. 25^v–31^v of X are set out on facing pages with D on the left-hand page. The manuscript page or folio reference is shown in the margin of each page, and manuscript page or folio boundaries are incorporated within the text within square brackets (e.g. samlæredan, [p. 98] ac gebete). The division of the text into separate numbered sections is based on the (unnumbered) paragraphing of D; sections which appear in X only are distinguished by the presence of an opening formula (*and riht is*; *and gyf*). The numbering of the sections is serial, following those sections which are judged by the editor to be 'authentic' on the basis of their sources, style, etc. Interpolated sections take the number of the previous authentic section, followed by a lower-case letter (e.g. 68a). Because several new sections are admitted to authenticity, the numbering departs from that of Thorpe and Jost: where this happens, towards the end, reference to Jost is given in parentheses after the section number (e.g. 68 (Jost 65)). Sections which occur in one manuscript only are paralleled by blank spaces on the opposite page.

Abbreviations have been expanded silently, following the Society's policy in this matter. All are standard and employed fairly regularly. Examples of the more common marks of abbreviation may be seen in the frontispiece, which corresponds to Sections 33–42 of the text. The Latin glosses in X, often almost illegible, are heavily abbreviated, but quite conventionally; again, examples may be seen in the frontispiece. All glosses printed in the textual notes are in hand 1 (see pp. xiii–xiv, above) unless otherwise identified; sometimes the hand cannot be determined and I have had to record a query—?

THE CANONS OF EDGAR

Corpus 201

p. 97   HER GEBIRAÐ NU TO EADGARES GERÆDNES
BE GEHADODRA MANNA LIFFADUNGE

1. We lærað þæt Godes þeowas beon geornlice Gode þeowigende and þenigende and for eal cristen folc þingigende; and þæt hi ealle beon a heora ealdre holde and gehyrsume, and ealle anræde to gemænre þearfe; and þæt ælc sy oðrum to fultume and helpe ge for Gode ge for worlde; and þæt hi beon heora worldhlafordum eac holde and getrywe.

2. And we lærað þæt ælc wurðige oðerne; and hyran þa gingran georne heora yldrum, and lufian and læran þa yldran georne heora gingran.

3. And we lærað þæt hi to ælcon sinoðe habban ælce geare becc and reaf to godcundre þenunge, and blæc and bocfel to heora gerædnessum, and þreora daga biwiste.

4. And we lærað þæt preosta gehwilc to sinoðe hæbbe his cleric and gefædne man to cnihte, and nænigne unwitan þe disig lufige; ac faran ealle mid gefæde and mid Godes ælmihtiges ege.

5. And we lærað þæt ælc preost on sinoðe gecyðe gif heom hwæt derige, and gif him ænig man healice misboden hæbbe; and fon hi þonne ealle on swilce hit heom eallum gedon beo, and gefilstan to þæt hit man gebete swa biscop getæce.

6. And we lærað þæt preosta gehwilc on synoðe gecyðe gif he on his scriftscire ænigne man wite Gode oferhyre, oððe on heafodleahtrum yfele befealenne, þe he to bote gebigan ne mæge oððe ne durre for worldafole.

7 And we lærað þæt nan sacu þe betweox preostan sy ne beo gescoten to worldmanna some, ac seman and sibbian heora agenne geferan, oððe sceotan to ðam biscope gif man þæt nyde scule.

Heading] GEHADODRA MANNA *altered from* GEHADODUM MANNUM

XX ITEM SINODALIA DECRETA

1. Riht is þæt preostas beon geornlice Gode þeowiende and ðeniende and for eall cristen folc ðingiende; and þæt hig ealle beon a heora ealdre holde and gehyrsume, and ealle anræde to gemænre þearfe; and þæt ælc sy oðrum on fultume and on helpe ge for Gode ge for worulde; and þæt heo beon heora woruldhlafordum eac holde and getrywe æfter Godes rihte.

2. And riht is þæt ælc wurðie oðerne; and hyran þa gingran georne heora yldrum, and lufian and læran þa yldran georne heora gingran.

5. And riht is þæt preostas on sinoðe gecyðan gif heom hwæt derige, and gif heom ænig man healice misboden hæbbe; fon hi þonne ealle on swylce hit hym eallum gedon beo, and gefylstan to þæt man hit gebete [f. 26] swa se bisceop getæce.

6. And riht is þæt preosta gehwylc on sinode gecyðe gyf he on his scriftscyre ænine man wite Gode oferhyre, oþðon on heafodleahtrum yfele befallen, þe he to bote gebigean ne mæge oððe ne durre for woruldafole.

7. And riht is þæt nan sacu þe betweox preostum sy ne beo gescoten to woruldmanna some, ac seman and sibbian heora agene geferan, oððe sceoton to ðam bisceope gyf man nyde sceole.

1 *First five words in capitals in MS*   holde] *erasure between* h *and* o   gehyrsume] e *over* y *in hand?*   2 hyran] *glossed* obediant   yldrum, yldran] e *over* y *in hand?*   5 hym] a *over* y *in hand?*   getæce] *glossed* docet   6 wite] *glossed* sciat   Gode] *glossed* deo   oferhyre] *glossed* inobedientes   -leahtrum] *marked with three dots above for a gloss, but not glossed*   7 (woruldmanna) some] *glossed* congregatione   sceoton] *marked with three dots above for a gloss, but not glossed*

pp. 97-8 8. And we lærað þæt ænig preost silfwilles ne forlæte þa circan þe he to gebletsod wæs, ac hæbbe him þa to rihtæwe.

9. And we lærað þæt nan preost oðrum ne ætdo æni þara þinga þe him to gebirige: ne on hys mynstre, ne on his scriftscire, ne on his gildscipe, ne on ænig þara þinga þe hym to gebirige.

10. And we lærað þæt ænig preost ne underfo oðres scolere buton þæs leafe þe he ær folgode.

11. And we lærað þæt preosta gehwilc toeacan lare leornige handcræft georne.

12. And we lærað þæt ænig gelæred preost ne scænde þone samlæredan, [p. 98] ac gebete hine gif he bet cunne.

13. And we lærað þæt ænig forðboren preost ne forseo þone læsborenan; gif man hit ariht asmeað, þonne syn ealle men anra gebirda.

14. And we lærað þæt preosta gehwilc tilige him rihtlice, and ne beo ænig mangere mid unrihte ne gitsigende massere.

15. And we lærað þæt preosta gehwilc fulluhtes tiðige sona swa man his girne, and æghwar on his scriftscire beode þæt ælc cild sy gefullod binnon xxxvii nihtum and þæt ænig man to lange unbiscopod ne wurðe.

16. And we lærað þæt preosta gehwilc cristendom geornlice arære and ælcne hæþendom mid ealle adwæsce; and forbeode wilweorþunga, and licwiglunga, and hwata, and galdra, and manweorðunga, and þa gemearr ðe man drifð on mistlicum gewiglungum and on friðsplottum and on ellenum, and eac on oðrum mistlicum treowum and on stanum, and on manegum mistlicum gedwimerum þe men on dreogað fela þæs þe hi na ne scoldan.

---

14 gitsigende] s *written through* t   16 forbeode] *Jost* (Polity, *p. 184*) *reads* forbeade *and comments* 'Eher forbeade *als* forbeode'. *In fact, the original misspelling* a *has been carefully altered to* o *by the scribe*

8. And riht is þæt ænig preost sylfwilles ne forlæte þa cyrican þe ff. 26-6ᵛ
he to gebletsod wæs, ac hæbbe þa him to rihtæwe.

9. And riht is þæt nan preost oðrum ne ætdo ænig þæra þinga þe
him to gebyrige: ne on his mynstre, ne on his scriftscire, ne on his
gyldscipe, ne on ænigum þæra ðinga þe him to gebyrige.

10. And riht is þæt ænig preost ne underfo scole butan þæs leafe
þe he ær folgade.

11. And riht is þæt preosta gehwylc toeacan lare leornige handcræft georne.

12. And riht is þæt ænig gelæred preost ne scende þone samlæredan, ac gebete hine [f. 26ᵛ] gif he bet cunne.

13. And riht is þæt ænig forðboren preost ne forseo þone læsborenan; forðam gif hit man ariht asmeaþ, þonne syn ealle men anra
gebyrda.

14. And riht is þæt preosta gehwylc tylige him rihtlice, and ne beo
ænig mangeara mid unrihte ne gytsiende massere.

15. And riht is þæt preosta gehwylc fulluhtes and scriftes tyðige
sona swa man gyrne, and æghwær on his scriftscyre beode þæt ælc
cild sy gefullod binnon vii nihtum and þæt ænig man to lange
unbiscopad ne wyrðe.

16. And riht is þæt preosta gehwylc cristendom geornlice lære and
ælcne hæþendom mid ealle adwæsce; and forbeode wyllweorðunga,
and licwigelunga, and hwata, and galdra, and treowwurðunga, and
stanwurðunga, and ðone deofles cræft þe man dryhð þær man þa
cild þurh þa eorðan tihð, and ða gemearr þe man drihð on geares
niht on mislicum wigelungum and on friðsplottum and on ellenum,
and on manegum mislicum gedwimerum þe men on dreogað fela
þæs þe hi ne sceoldan. [f. 27]

   8 forlæte] *glossed* deferat   rihtæwe] *glossed* uxore *in hand 2*   *after* rihtæwe,
in margin] þa hwile þe his lif sig *in hand 3*   10 *above* scole] oðres ... re *in
hand 3 (cf.* D*10*)   12 samlæredan] *glossed* semidoctum   13 syn] d *written
above* n *in darker ink*   anra gebyrda] *glossed* natalicie unius   14 mangeara]
written man geara, *with the first* a *of* geara *partly erased*   massere] *glossed* mercator   15 tyðige] *glossed* concedat   beode] *glossed* iubeat
16 wyll-] *glossed* fontis   -weorðunga] *glossed* uenerationem   hwata] *glossed* omen
ellenum] *glossed* eluene *in hand 2. This context of a discussion of heathen practices has suggested 'elves' to the glossator. This is the only real error among the
glosses* gedwimerum] *glossed* fantasiis   dreogað] *glossed* þolieð

pp. 98-9 17. And we lærað þæt ælc cristen man his bearn to cristendome geornlice wænige, and him pater noster and credon tæce.

18. And we lærað þæt man geswice freolsdagum hæþenra leoða and deofles gamena.

19. And we lærað þæt man geswice sunnandæges cypinge and folcgemota.

20. And we lærað þæt man geswice higeleasra ræda and dislicra geræda, and bismorlicra efesunga.

21. And we lærað þæt man geswice cifesgemana[n] and lufige rihtæwe.

22. And we lærað þæt ælc man leornige þæt he cunne pater noster and credon, be þam þe he wille on gehalgodan licgan oððe husles wyrðe beon; forðam he ne bið wel cristen þe* þæt geleornian nele, ne he nah mid rihte oðres mannes to onfonne æt fulluhte ne æt biscopes handa, se þe þæt ne cann, ær he hit geleornige.

23. And we lærað þæt freolsdagum and rihtfæstendagum æni geflit ne beo betweox mannum ealles to swiðe.

24. And we lærað þæt man freolsdagum and fæstendagum forga aðas and ordela.

25. And we lærað þæt ælc wer forga his wif freolstidum and rihtfæstentidum.

26. And we lærað þæt preostas cirican healdan mid ealre arwurð-nesse to godcundre þenunge and to clænan þeowdome, and to nanum oðrum þingum; ne hi þar ænig unnit inne ne on neawesté ne geþafian: ne idele spæce, ne idele dæde, ne unnit gedrync, ne æfre ænig idel; ne binnan cirictune ænig hund ne cume, ne swyn þe ma, þæs þe man wealdan mæge.

27. And we lærað þæt man into circan ænig þingc ne logige [p. 99] þæs þe þarto ungedafenlic sy.

---

21 cifesgemana] *something has been almost completely erased between the* n *and* a. *The emendation, which puts the word in the genitive, follows Jost* (Polity, *p. 186*)
22 *after* gehalgodan] legere *inserted above*   * *the scribe first wrote* þ, *erased it, and wrote* þe *over the erasure*

17. And riht is þæt ælc cristen man his bearn to cristendome ff. 27-7ᵛ
geornlice wenige, and him pater noster and credan getæce.

18. And riht is þæt man geswice freolsdagum hæðenra leoða and
deofles gamena.

19. And riht is þæt man geswice sunnandæges cypincge.

20. And riht is þæt man geswice higleasra wæda and dyslicra
geræda, and bysmorlicra efesunge.

22. And riht is þæt ælc man leornige þæt he cunne pater noster
and credan, be ðam þe he wille on gehalgodum licgan oþðon
husles wyrðe beon; forðam he ne bið wel cristen þe þæt geleornian
nele, ne he nah mid rihte oðres mannes to onfonne æt fulluhte ne
æt bisceopes handa, se ðe þæt ne can, ær he hit geleornige.

23. And riht is þæt freolsdagum and rihtfæstendagum ænig geflit
ne beo betweox mannum.

24. And riht is þæt man freolsdagum and rihtfæstendagum forga
aþas and ordela.

25. And riht is þæt ælc wer forga his wif freolstidum and rihtfæstentidum.

26. And riht is þæt preostas cyrican healdan mid ealre arwyrðnysse
to godcundre þenunge and to clænan þeowdome, and to nanum
oðrum þingum; ne hy þær ænig [f. 27ᵛ] unnyt inne ne on neaweste
ne geþafian: ne idele spæce, ne idele dæde, ne unnyt gedryh, ne
æfre ænig idel; ne binnan cyrictune ænig hund ne hors ne cume,
ne swyn þe ma, þæs þe man wealdan mæge.

27. And riht is þæt man into cyrican ænig þing ne logie þæs þe
þærto ungedafenlic sy.

<small>18 *after* freolsdagum, *above the line*] æt cyrcan *added in hand 4*   gamena] *glossed*
custodiant, *and crossed out. The glossator has confused* gamena *with* gemene
20 *before* wæda] ge *inserted in hand 4*   *after* efesunge] oððe unefesunge *added
in hand 4*   26 cyrican] h *above each* c, *apparently in hand 1*   gedryh] þa
suffixed in hand ?   cyrictune] *glossed* cimiterio; h *above each* c   *in margin*]
andreas   27 logie] *glossed* ponat   ungedafenlic] *glossed* indecens</small>

28. And we lærað þæt man æt ciricwæccan swiðe gedreoh sy, and georne gebidde, and æni gedrenc ne ænig unnit þar ne dreoge.

29. And we lærað þæt man innan circan ænigne man ne birige bute man wite þæt he on life Gode to ðam wel gecweme þæt man þurh þæt læte þæt he sy þæs legeres wyrðe.

30. And we lærað þæt preost on ænigum huse ne mæssige buton on gehalgodre cirican, buton hit sy for hwilces mannes oferseocneses.

31. And we lærað þæt preost huru æfre ne mæssige buton onufan gehalgodon weofode.

32. And we lærað þæt preost æfre ne mæssige buton bec; ac beo se canon him ætforan eagum. Beseo to gif he wille, þi læs þe him misse.

33. And we lærað þæt ælc preost habbe corporalem þonne he mæssige and subumlem under his alban, and eal mæssereaf wurðlice behworfen.

34. And we lærað þæt ælc preost georne tilige þæt he gode and huru rihte becc hæbbe.

35. And we lærað þæt ænig mæssepreost ana ne mæssige þæt he næbbe þone þe hym acweðe.

36. And we lærað þæt ænig unfæstende man husles ne abirige, buton hit for oferseocnesse sy.

37. And we lærað þæt ænig preost anes dæges oftor ne mæssige þonne þrywa mæst þara þynga.

38. And we lærað þæt preost hæbbe a geara husl þam þe þearf sy, and þæt georne on clænnesse healde, and warige þæt hit na forealdige. Gif hit þonne forhealden sy, þæt his man brucan ne mæge, þonne forbærne hit man on clænum fire, and þa axsan under weofode gebringe, and bete wið God georne se þe hit forgimde.

38 under] *MS.* unde

JUNIUS 121

28. And riht is þæt man æt cyricwæccan swyðe dreoh sy, and ff. 27ᵛ-8
georne gebidde, and ænig gedrync ne ænig unnytt ðær ne dreoge.

29. And riht is þæt man innan cyrican ænine man ne byrige butan
man wite þæt he on life Gode to ðam wel gecwemde þæt man þurh
þæt læte þæt he sy þæs legeres wyrðe.

30. And riht is þæt ænig preost on ænigum huse ne mæssige butan
on gehalgodre cyrican, butan hyt sy for hwilces mannes oferseocnesse.

31. And riht is þæt preost æfre ne mæssige butan onufan gehalgodum weofode.

32. And riht is þæt preost æfre ne mæssige butan bec; ac beo se
canon him ætforan eagum. Beseo to gyf he wylle, þæ læste him
misse.

33. And riht is þæt ælc preost hæbbe corporale þonne he mæssige
and subumbrale under his alban, and eall mæsse[f. 28]reaf wurðlice behworfen.

34. And riht is þæt ælc preost tylige georne þæt he gode and huru
rihte bec hæbbe.

35. And riht is þæt ænig mæssepreost ana ne mæssige; þæt he
hæbbe þone þe him acweðe.

36. And riht is þæt ænig unfæstende man husles ne abyrige, butan
hit for oferseocnysse sy.

37. And riht is þæt ænig preost anes dæges oftor ne mæssige þonne
þriwa mæstra ðinga.

38. And riht is þæt preost a geara husel hæbbe þam þe þearf sy,
and þæt georne on clænnysse healde, and warnige þæt hit ne
forealdige. Gyf ðonne hit forhealden sy, þæt his man brucan ne
mæge, þonne forbærne hit man on clænum fyre, and ða axan under
weofode gebringe, and bete wið God georne se ðe hit forgyme.

    28 cyricwæccan] h *above last* c   dreoh] ge *prefixed in hand 4?*   sy] beo *above in hand 4?*   29 cyrican] h *above second* c   Gode] *glossed* deo   læte] *glossed* iudicet
30 butan ... oferseocnesse] *crossed out by a single thin stroke*   32 butan] *glossed* sine   þæ ... misse] þu lest he misse *in margin*   34 gode] *glossed* bonos
36 abyrige] *glossed* gustet   37 *A small cross appears over the beginning of this section. Cf.* 40 *and* 41   þriwa] *crossed out and* twiga *written above in hand 4*
38 *above the second* þæt] h (?) *in hand 1?*   warnige] *glossed* caueat   brucan] *glossed* frui *in hand 1?*   forgyme] e *over* y. *Cf.* 1, 2, 42, 43

pp. 99-100 39. And we lærað þæt næfre preost ne geþristlæce þæt he mæssige buton he eal hæbbe þæt to husle gebirige: þæt is clæne oflete, and clæne win, and clæne wæter. Wa ðam þe mæssian onginð buton he ælc þara habbe, and wa ðam þe þar ful þing todeð þonne gelice þam þe Iudeas didon þa hi mængdon eced and geallan togædere and hit siððan on bismer Criste gebudon.

40. And we lærað þæt æfre ne gewurðe þæt preost mæssige and silf þæt husl ne geþicge, ne man gehalgod næfre eft halgige.

41. And we lærað þæt ælc calic gegoten beo þe man husl on halgige, and on treowenum ne halgige man ænig.

42. And we lærað þæt ealle þa þingc þe weofode neah beon and to circan gebirgan beon swiðe clænlice and wurðlice behworfene, and þar ænig þingc neah ne cume; ac geloge man þone haligdom swiðe arwurðlice. And a sy byrnende leoht [p. 100] on circan þonne man mæssan singe.

43. And we lærað þæt man ne forgime ænig gehalgod þingc: ne halig wæter, ne sealt, ne stor, ne hlaf, ne ænig þingc haliges.

44. And we lærað þæt æni wifman neah weofode ne cume þa hwile þe man mæssige.

45. And we lærað þæt man on rihtne timan tida ringe, and preosta gehwilc ðonne his tidsang on circan gesece, and þar mid Godes ege hig georne gebiddan and for eal folc ðingian.

46. And we lærað þæt mæssepreosta oððe mynsterpreosta ænig ne cume binnan circan dyre ne binnan weohstealle buton his oferslipe, ne huru æt þam weofode þæt he þar þenige buton þare wæde.

45 for] *a much elongated* r *has been added by another hand to complete this word*
46 mynsterpreosta] *the second* s *supplied by another hand*

39. And riht is þæt preost æfre ne geþristlæce þæt he mæssige ff. 28–9
butan he eall hæbbe þæt to husle gebyrige: þæt his [sic] clæne
oflete, and clæne win, and clæne wæter. Wa þam þe mæssan onginð
butan he ælc þara hæbbe, and wa þam þe þær ful to deð: forðam he
deð þonne gelice þam ðe Iudeas dydon þa hi mengdon eced and
geallan togædere and hit syððan on bysmor [f. 28ᵛ] Criste gebudon.

40. And riht is þæt æfre ne geweorðe þæt preost mæssige and sylf
þæt husel ne þicge, ne man gehalgod husel æfre eft halgige.

41. And riht is þæt ælc calic gegoten beo þe man husel on halgige,
and on treowenum ne halgige man ænig; ne nænne man fullige
oftor þonne æne.

42. And riht is þæt ealle þa ðing þe weofode neah beon and to
cyrcan gebyrian beon swyðe clænlice and wurðlice behworfene,
and ðær ænig þing fules neah ne cume; ac gelogige man þone
haligdom swyðe arwurðlice. And a sy byrnende leoht on cyrican
þonne man mæssan singe.

43. And riht is þæt man ne forgyme ænig gehalgod þing: ne halig
wæter, ne sealt, ne stor, ne hlaf, ne gehalgode axan, ne gehalgod
oft, ne ænig þing haliges. Ac forbærne hit man on clænum fyre,
butan his man elles notian mæge, and ða axan under weofode
gebringe.

44. And riht is þæt ænig wifman neah weofode ne cume þa hwile
þe man mæssige.

45. And riht is þæt man on rihtne timan tida hrincge, and preosta
gehwylc þonne his tidsang [f. 29] on cyrcan gesece, and ðær mid
Godes ege hi georne gebiddan and for eall folc þingian.

46. And riht is þæt mæssapreosta nan ne cume gewæpned binnan
cyrican dura, ne binnan weofodstealle butan his oferslope, ne huru
æt ðam weofode þæt he þær þenige butan þære wæde.

39 geþristlæce] *glossed* presumat   Wa] *glossed* ve   ful] *glossed* fetidum *after* forðam] þe *inserted above in hand ?*   eced] *glossed* eisil *in hand 2?*
40 *There is a small cross over the beginning of this section*   41 beo *has a small cross above it, which refers to a marginal addition in hand 4:* Gylden oððe seolfren tinen   ænig] *an interlinear addition in hand 4 starts above this word:* Gif he nylle beon amansumad; *this should refer to* 40: *see p. 34 below*   42 byrnende] e *above* y   43 forgyme] e *above* y   oft] e *written above this corrupt form to give* ofet '*fruit*', *glossed* frut *in margin in hand?*   Ac] *the* A *is a capital in the MS.; this sentence is not in* D   46 butan] *glossed* sine

p. 100 47. And we lærað þæt ænig gehadod man his scare ne helige, ne hine misefesian læte, ne his beard ænige hwile hæbbe, be þam þe he wille Godes bletsunge habban and sancte Petres and ure.

48. And we lærað þæt ealle preostas æt freolsan and æt fæstenan anræde beon, and ealle on ane wisan beodan þæt hi folc ne dwelian.

49. And we lærað þæt ælc fæsten beo mid ælmessan gewurðad, þæt is þæt gehwa on Godes est ælmessan georne sille: þonne bið his fæsten Gode þe gecwemre.

50. And we lærað þæt preostas on ciricþenungum ealle an dreogan, and beon efenweorðe on geares fæce on eallum ciricþenungum.

51. And we lærað þæt preostas geoguðe geornlice læran, and to cræftan teon, þæt hi ciricfultum habban.

52. And we lærað þæt preostas ælce sunnandæge folce bodigan and aa wel bisnian.

53. And we lærað þæt nan cristen man blod ne þicge.

54. And we lærað þæt preostas folc mynegian þæs þe hig Gode don sculan to gerihtan on teoðungum and on oðrum þingum: ærest sulhælmessan xv niht onufan eastron, and geoguðe teoðunge be pentecosten, and eorðwestma be omnium sanctorum, and Romfeoh be Petres mæssan, and ciricsceat be Martinus mæssan.

55. And we lærað þæt preostas swa dælan folces ælmessan þæt hig ægðer don ge God gegladian ge folc to ælmessan gewænian.

48 beodan] *the scribe first wrote* beon *and altered it to* beodan *before he wrote* þæt   51 læran *was first written* lære *and then altered by the original scribe; cf.* 48 beodan   53 nanes cynnys or[f] *is added at the end of the line in a large untidy hand which becomes illegible after* or: *on the emendation, see Commentary. The same hand appears to have supplied* nan *over an erasure (cf. X53* ænig), *added four heavy curved accents (over* nan, blod, nanes, *and* cynnys) *and perhaps supplied the final* n *of* don *in 54, which appears at the end of the line immediately below the addition to 53 and also has a large accent*   54 be (Martinus mæssan) *has* to *written above it in the original hand*

47. And riht is þæt ænig gehadod mann his sceare ne helige, ne ff. 29-9ᵛ
hine misefesian ne læte, ne his beard ænige hwile hæbbe, be þam
þe he wille Godes bletsunga habban and sancte Petres and ure.

48. And riht is þæt ealle preostas æt freolsan and æt fæstenan
anræde beon, and ealle on ane wisan beodan þæt hi folc ne dwelian.

49. And riht is þæt ælc fæsten beo mid ælmessan gewurðod, þæt
is þæt gehwa on Godes est ælmessan georne sylle: þonne bið his
fæsten Gode gecweme.

50. And riht is þæt preostas on cyricþenungum ealle an dreogan,
and beon efenforðe ofer geares fæc on eallum cyricþenungum.

51. And riht is þæt preostas geogoðe geornlice læran, and to cræftum teon, þæt hy cyricfultum habban.

52. And riht is þæt preostas ælce sunnandæge folce bodian and a
wel [f. 29ᵛ] bysnian.

53. And riht is þæt ænig cristen man blod ne þycge.

54. And riht is þæt preostas folc mynegian þæs þe hi Gode don
sculon to gerihtum on teoþungum and on oðrum þingum. And
riht is þæt man þisses mynegige to eastrum, oðre siðe to gangdagum, þriddan siðe to middan sumera þonne bið mæst folces
gegaderod. Ærest sulhælmessan xv niht ofer eastran, geogoðe
teoðunge be pentecosten, Romfeoh be Petres mæssan, eorðwæstma
be ealra halgena mæssan, cyricsceat to Martinus mæssan, and
leohtgesceotu þriwa on geare: ærest on easter æfen, and oðre siðe
on candelmæsse æfen, þriddan siðe on ealra halgena mæsse æfen.

55. And riht is þæt preostas swa dælan folces ælmessan þæt hi
ægðer don ge God gegladian ge folc to ælmessan wenian.

56 (Jost note to 55, p. 200). And riht is þæt man betæce ænne dæl
preostum, oþerne dæl to cyricneode, þriddan dæl þam þearfum.

48 anræde] *glossed* constantes   49 est] *glossed* deuotione   50 an] *glossed*
vnum   fæc] *glossed* spacium   51 geogoðe] *glossed* iuuenes   53 þycge]
glossed gustet   54 Gode] *glossed* deo   oðre] *glossed* iterum   sulh-] *glossed*
suluh *in hand* 2 ?

pp. 100-1 57 (Jost 56).* And we lærað þæt preostas sealmas singan þonne hi ða ælmessan dælan, and þa þearfan georne biddan þæt hig for þæt folc þingian.

58 (Jost 57). And we lærað þæt preostas beorgan wið oferdruncen and hit georne belean oðrum mannum.

59 (Jost 58). And we lærað þæt ænig preost ne beo ealascop, ne on ænige wisan gliwige mid him silfum oðrum mannum, ac beo swa his had[e] [p. 101] gebirað, wis and weorðfull.

60 (Jost 59). And we lærað þæt preostas wið aðas beorgan him georne, and hig eac swiðe forbeodan.

61 (Jost 60). And we lærað þæt ænig preost ne lufige wifmanna neawyste ealles to swiðe, ac lufige his rihtæwe, þæt is his cirice.

62 (Jost 61). And we lærað þæt æni preost ne stande on leasre gewitnesse, ne þeofa gewita beon.

63 (Jost 62). And we lærað þæt preost bisæce ordol æfre ne geæðe.

64 (Jost 63). And we lærað þæt preost wið þegn ne ladige buton þegnes foraðe.

65 (Jost 64). And we lærað þæt preost ne beo hunta ne hafecere ne tæflere, ac plegge on his bocum swa his hade gebirað.

68 (Jost 65). And we lærað þæt ælc preost scrife and dædbote tæce þam þe him andette, and eac to bote filste, and seoce men huslige

---

* As my numbering departs from that of Jost (Polity, pp. 178-209) from this point on, I give his numbering in parentheses   59 had[e]] final e and part of d almost rubbed away   62 gewita] the scribe wrote gewitu and then altered the final letter   beon] so MS.; Jost beo

57 (Jost 56). And riht is þæt preostas sealmas singan þonne hy ða ff. 29ᵛ-30ᵛ
ælmessan dælan, and ða þearfan georne biddan þæt hi for þæt
[f. 30] folc þingian.

58 (Jost 57). And riht is þæt preostas beorgen wið oferdruncen and
hit georne belean oðrum mannum.

59 (Jost 58). And riht is þæt ænig preost ne beo ealusceop, ne on
ænige wisan gliwige mid him sylfum oðrum mannum, ac beo swa
his hade gebyrað, wis and weorðfull.

60 (Jost 59). And riht is þæt preostas wið aþas beorgan heom
georne, and hi eac swyþe forbeodan.

62 (Jost 61). And riht is þæt ænig preost ne stande on leasre
gewitnesse, ne þeofa gewita beo.

63 (Jost 62). And riht is þæt preost bisæce ordol æfre ne geæþe.

64 (Jost 63). And riht is þæt preost wið þegen ne ladige butan
þegenes foraþe.

65 (Jost 64). And riht is þæt preost ne beo hunta ne hafecere ne
tæflere, ac plege on his bocum swa his hade gebyrað. (Jost note
to his 64, p. 202) Se canon segð gyf hwylc gehadod man on huntaþ
fare, gyf hit bið clerec forga xii monað flæsc, diacon twa gear,
mæssepreost þreo, bisceop vii.

66 (Jost note to his 64, p. 202). And gyf hwylc bisceop oððe mæssepreost oððe ænig gehadod man hine sylfne rædlice oferdrince,
oððe he þæs geswice, oððe his hades þolige.

67 (Cf. this edition, D and X 69; Jost X64a). And riht is þæt
preostas aa gearuwe beon to folces gerihtum.

68 (Jost 65). And riht is þæt ælc preost scrife and dædbote tæce
þam þe him [f. 30ᵛ] andette, and eac to bote fylste, and seoce men

58 beorgen] *glossed* caueantur   belean] *glossed* forbeoden *in hand 2*
59 gliwige] *glossed* ludat *in hand ?*   oðrum] þ *above in hand ?. Cf.* 66   60 wið]
glossed contra *in hand 1?*   62 gewita] *glossed* testis   65 hafecere] *dotted
for erasure below* ce, *with* ca *above in hand ?*   plege] *glossed* ludat *in hand ?*
66 rædlice] *glossed* scienter   oððe . . . oððe] þ . . . þ *above in hand ?*

p. 101 þonne heom þearf si, and hi eac smerige gif hi þæs girnan, and æfter forðsiðe georne behweorfe, and ne geþafige ænig unnitt æt þam lice, ac hit mid Godes ege wislice bebirge.

huslige þonne heom þearf sy, and eac hy smyrige gif hi þæs gyrnan, ff. 30ᵛ-1
and æfter forðsiðe georne behweorfe, and ne geþafige ænig unnytt
æt þam lice, ac hit mid Godes ege wislice bebyrge.

68a (cf. this edition D61; Jost X65a). And riht is þæt ænig preost
ne lufige wifmanna neawiste ealles to swiþe, ac lufige his rihtæwe,
þæt is his cyrice.

68b (Jost X65b). And riht is gif weofodþen his agen lif be boca
tæcincge rihtlice fadige, þonne sy he fulles þegnscipes wyrþe ge
on life ge on legere. Gyf he his lif misfadige, wanige his wyrðscipe
be ðam þe seo dæd sy. Wite, gif he wylle, ne gebyrað him naðor ne
to wife ne to woruldwige, gif he Gode wile rihtlice hyran and Godes
lage rihtlice healdan.

68c (Jost X65c). Dunstan gedemde þæt se mæssepreost nære, gif
he wif hæfde, ænige oðre lade wyrþe butan eallswa læwede sceolde
þe efenboren wære, gif man mid tihtlan þæne belede.

68d (Jost X65d). And riht is gyf weofodþen hine hrihtlice [sic]
healde, þonne sy he fulles weres and wurðscipes wyrðe.

68e (Jost X65e–f). And gyf hit [f. 31] gewurðe þæt man mid tihtlan
and mid uncræftum sacerd belecge þe regollice libbe, and he hine
sylfne wite þas clæne, mæssige gyf he durre, and ladige on þam
husle hine sylfne æt anfealdre spræce; æt ðryfealdre spræce ladige
gif he durre, eac on þam husle, mid twam his gehadan.

68f (Jost X65g–h). Gif man diacon tihtlige, þe regollice libbe,
anfealdre spræce, nime twegen his gehadan and ladige hine mid
þam; and gif man hine tihtlige ðryfealdre spræce, nime six his
gehadan and ladige mid þam, and beo he sylf seofeða.

68g (Jost X65i). And gif man folciscne mæssepreost mid tihtlan
belecge þe regollif næbbe, ladige hine swa diacon þe regollife libbe.

68 þam lice] *something has been erased between these two words, leaving a space for about two letters*   68a riht-] *glossed* legem *in hand* 2?; *the gloss is actually written over* -æwe   -æwe] *glossed* coniugem; *the gloss is in the margin*   68b fadige] *glossed* lede *in hand* 2?   (mis)fadige] *glossed* let *in hand* ?   (woruld)wige] *glossed* prelio   hyran] *glossed* pavere   68c *Modern English glosses begin here and continue sporadically through the rest of the text*   ænige] r *inserted between* g *and* e *in another hand*   68e tihtlan] *glossed* ortationibus suggestionibus   belecge] *glossed* mentitur   þe] *glossed* qui *in hand* 1?

69 (Jost 66). And we læraðþæt preosta gehwilc ægðer hæbbe ge fulluhtele ge seocum smyrels, and eac geara sy to folces gerihtum, and cristendom firðrige georne on æghwilce wisan, and ægðer do ge wel bodige ge wel bisnige. Þonne geleanað him þæt ælmihtig God swa hym leofost bið.

70 (Jost 67). And we læraðþæt ælc preost wite to cyðanne, þonne he crisman fecce, hwæt he on gebedum for cyngc and biscop gedon hæbbe.

70 *The heading for* Geðyncðo (BE WERGILDUM AND BE GEÐINÐUM) (*ed.* Gesetze, *I, 456–8*) *follows immediately on from Canons 70, on the same line*

68h (Jost X65k). And gyf man freondleasne weofodþen mid tihtlan ff. 31–31ᵛ
belecge þe aðfultum næbbe, ga to corsnæde, and ðær þonne æt
gefare þæt þæt God wylle, butan he on husle ladian mote.

68i (Jost X65l–m). And gif man gehadodne mid fæhðe belecge, and
secge þæt he wære dædbana, ladige mid his magum þe fæhða motan
mid beran oððe fore betan. [f. 31ᵛ] And gyf he sy mægleas, ladige
mid geferan oððe on fæsten fo, gif he þæt þurfe, and ga to corsnæde,
and þæræt gefare swa swa God ræde.

69 (Jost 66). And riht is þæt preosta gehwylc ægþer hæbbe ge
fulluhtele ge seocum smerels, and a gearu sy to folces gerihtum,
and cristendom fyrðrige georne on æghwylce wisan, and ægðer do
ge wel bodige ge wel bysnige. Þonne geleanað him þæt God ælmihtig swa him leofost bið. Amen.

68h belecge] *a gloss above this word has been almost completely erased*   68i
magum] *glossed* meies *in hand 2*   betan] *Jost* (Polity, *p. 208*) *comments that the* b
has been corrected from þ *by erasure; actually, it is a heavy* 7 *showing through from*
31ᵛ *which gives the impression of the descender of a* þ *below* b

APPENDIX I

THE TEXT OF CANONS OF EDGAR 1, 2, 5-8 IN CAMBRIDGE UNIVERSITY LIBRARY, MS. ADD. 3206 (CU)

As noted in the Introduction, this fragment has been mutilated and has lost about three letters at the end of each line, and the bottom half of the last line. The text given below has been reconstructed by comparison with X. The orthographic conventions of the fragment itself are followed in the emendations where the conventions are consistent enough to be a guide.

Cu p. 4

1. Riht is ðæt preostas beon geornlice Gode þeowiend[e and] þeniende and for eal cristen folc þingiende; and þæt hi ealle b[eon] a heora ealdre holde and hersume, and ealle anræde to g[emæn]re þearfe; and þæt elc si oþrum on fultume and on helpe ge for G[ode] ge for worolde; and þæt he beon heora woruldhlafordum e[ac holde] and getreowe æfter Godes rihte.

2. And riht is þæt elc wurðige o[þerne]; and hyran þa gingran georne heora yldran, and lufian and l[æran] þa yldran georne heora gingran.

5. And riht is þæt preostas [on sinoþe] gecyðan gif heom hwæt derige, and gif heom ænig man heali[ce mis]boden hæbbe; fon hi þonne ealle on swilce hit heom eall[um ge]don beo, and gefylstan to þæt man hit gebete swa se bis[ceop] getæce.

6. And riht is þæt preosta gehwilc on sinoþe gecyðe gif [he on his] scriftscire ænigne man wite Gode oferhyre, oþþon [on hea]fordleahtrum [*sic*] yfele befeallen, þe he to bote gebige[an ne] mage oþþe ne durre for woroldafole.

7. And riht is þæt n[an] sacu þe betweox preostum sy ne be gescoten to worold[man]na some, ac seman and sibbian heora agene ge[fe]ran, oþþ[e] sceotan to þam bisceope gif man nyde scyle.

8. And riht is þæt æ[nig preost sylfwilles ne forlæte þa circan þe he to geb]

---

1 First three words in capitals   6 [hea]fordleahtrum] *the* -ford- *suggests that the scribe may have misunderstood the word and written* hlafordleahtrum, *but I have amended according to X*

APPENDIX II

THE TEXT OF BRUSSELS, BIBLIOTHÈQUE ROYALE MS. 8558-63 (2498), F. 140

This corrupt text parallels certain sections of the *Canons* and the *Northumbrian Priests' Law*, as indicated in the footnotes below.

Bx f. 140

Gyf mæsseprest his agen lif rihtlice fadie, ðonne is riht þæt his wurðscipe wexe.[1] And gyf he elles do, gebete þæt georne swa swa hit heræfter tæcð. Þæt is ærest: gyf he his cirice miswurðige ðe eal his wurscipe is on belang, gebete þæt beo biscopes dome;[2] oððe he cilde fulwihtes forwerne, oððe scrifte ðam ðe neod beo, and he on ðam geændie,[3] ðonne beoð þæt micel pliht ðam ðe hit ongelang beoð, forðam se ænde hit eal belucað. Forðam ic bidde on Godes namen ælc ðare manne swiðe georne þe ðonne had habbe, and him ðærto geberige, þæt he ðas boc gelome on hande habbe him selfen to helpe and eallen ðam ðe he wissien scæl. And Ic bidde on Drihtenes namen ealle ða ðe presthad habbeð þæt ælc oðerne lufige mid rihte, and heren ða gingren georne here eldren, and læren ða eldren georne here gingren.[4] Ec we læreð preste gehwilcne ðeh he gehitte oþerne ðe swa wel ne cunne swa he scolde, þæt he nenne ne scænde, ac gebete hine luflice, gyf he bet cunne.[5] And we biddeð eac þæt nan forðboren prest ne forseo ðone læsborenen, forðam geof hit men on riht gesmeoð ðonne beo we ealle anre geberde.[6] And we læreð preste gehwilcne þæt he ealle criste men spette and spanne and ealle men hit eac understanden þæt næfre nan cristen man ne læte unandet nan ðare ðinge ðe he æfre geo dede, ðas ðe he geþencen mæg, þæt he don ne scollde. And æfre ælc prest berege, and to Gode gebidde, þæt he næfre on wimmannes bedde forð ne gewite.

wurscipe] ð *written above* r, *perhaps in the same hand is smudged, but appears to be this rather than* gesmeað

gesmeoð] *the word* næfre] r *written above* e

---

[1] Cf. *Canons* 68b.
[2] Cf. *Northumbrian Priests' Law* 25 (*Gesetze* I, 381).
[3] Cf. *Northumbrian Priests' Law* 8, 10. 1 (*Gesetze* I, 380, 381).
[4] Cf. *Canons* 2.   [5] Cf. *Canons* 12.   [6] Cf. *Canons* 13.

COMMENTARY

Heading D. It is difficult to account for the reference to Edgar, which has been a source of confusion since Thorpe's time. Jost's arguments in 'Einige Wulfstantexte' in 1932 made it impossible to accept a date as early as Edgar's reign.

We could regard the rubric as a misunderstanding by some scribe copying the manuscript—which is usually dated about the middle of the eleventh century—without knowing that the text was by Wulfstan. This is possible if, as seems likely, the manuscript was written in some place other than Worcester. Edgar II and III occur in D, and their presence may have suggested this rubric to the scribe. Another conjecture is that the rubric is a deliberate misrepresentation by Wulfstan or one of his scribes. Professor Whitelock has pointed out (*T.R.H.S.* xxiv, 1942) that Wulfstan admired Edgar: 'Wulfstan himself seems to have looked back on Edgar's reign as a golden age of law and order. See VIII Atr. 37 and ASC 975D. Perhaps there was a tendency in later times at Worcester to attribute undated codes to his reign.'

If we agree with R. R. Darlington's view of Wulfstan as a reforming bishop directly in the tradition of Dunstan, Ethelwold, and Oswald, he would have every reason to look back on Edgar's reign as a golden age, not only of law and order, but of progress in Church reform. Wulfstan made considerable use of II and III Edgar in the later codes of Ethelred and in both of Cnut's codes. IV Edgar occurs in one of the 'commonplacebook' MSS., C.C.C.C. 265, and contains material about the plague which could have influenced Wulfstan's view of the disastrous contemporary scene. In the version of the *Sermo Lupi* in MS. Hatton 113, contemporary disorder is contrasted with the situation before Edgar's death: *folclaga wyrsedan ealles to swyðe syððan Eadgar geendode*. Wulfstan may have been responsible for the revival of Edgar's laws mentioned in the D version of the *Chronicle* under 1018. These points are noted by Professor Bethurum (*Homilies*, pp. 82–3), whose general conclusion seems to be that the heading is Wulfstan's own, in view of his apparent admiration for Edgar and of the fact that 'the rubrics in (D) nearly always give reliable information'.

GEHADODRA MANNA LIFFADUNGE: but *Canons* 17–25 are phrased to apply to laymen as well as priests.

Heading X. xx is the number of the section in *Polity*. ITEM indicates that the subject is the same as that of the preceding section of *Polity*, which is headed *Be Sacerdum*. SINODALIA DECRETA perhaps refers back to an earlier section of *Polity*, x in the manuscript numbering, which is headed *Incipit de Synodo*. One is reminded of the fact that Wulfstan's main source, Ælfric's *Pastoral Letter to Wulfsige*, begins by setting out the decrees of the Synod of Nicaea. On synods in the Late OE. period see Darlington, op. cit., pp. 412–16.

COMMENTARY

1. **We lærað**: a common formula in Wulfstan: cf. Homily XV, 33, 36; VI Atr. 11; 1 Cn. 21, 22, 23, 25; II Cn. 2.

þeowigende ... þingigende: Cf. I *Pol.* 103 (II. 208): þeowian and þenian and for eal cristen folc þingian georne. Cf. Homily Xa, 8: þeowian 7 ðenian.

ealle ... þearfe: Cf. II *Pol.* 184: and weorðan anmode to gemænelicre þearfe.

and þæt ... getrywe (X æfter Godes rihte): Cf. Homily Xc, 165–6: Beo manna gehwylc hold 7 getrywe his worldhlaforde æfre mid rihte. The phrase *æfter Godes rihte* also occurs in II *Pol.* 19.

2. Cf. Homily Xc, 176–8: hyran þa gingran georne heora yldran, 7 lufian 7 læran þa yldran heora gingran. This is closer than Xa, 43–5: Ealde gebroðru lufian 7 læran georne heora gingran, 7 hyran þa gingran georne heora yldrum. Both Jost ('Einige Wulfstantexte', p. 304) and Professor Bethurum (*Homilies*, p. 103) date Xc immediately before the *Canons*, to which it is closely related in content. *Can.* 2, Xc, and Xb 136 reverse the order of clauses in Xa and the ultimate source, ch. 145 of Amalarius' *De Regula Canonicorum* (*PL* cv. 934): Seniores spiritaliter juniores diligant; juniores senioribus obsequium dignum exhibeant.

3. Cf. Theodulf, *Capitula* IV (*PL* cv. 193): Quando more solito ad synodum convenitis, vestimenta, et libros, et vasa sancta, cum quibus vestrum ministerium et injunctum officium peragitis, vobiscum deferte. Here, as in *Can.* 4, our text is more practical than the source, adding ink, parchment, and food. Jost, *Polity*, p. 219, prints a text *Be gehadedum mannum* (X, ff. 34–5ᵛ) which advises: gewarnige, þæt he hæbbe to þam fæce þa bigwiste on fodan and on foddre, þe he habban scule ...

4. Cf. Theodulf, ibid.: nec non duos, aut tres clericos, cum quibus missarum solemnia celebratis, vobiscum adducite, ut probetur quam diligenter, quam studiose Dei servitium peragatis.

Cf. *Incipit de Synodo* 6 (*Polity*, p. 212): Bisceopum gebyreð, þæt symle mid heom faran and mid heom wunian wel geþungene witan ...

5. That one of the functions of the synod was to settle grievances by corporate effort is borne out by a statement in *Polity*: Bisceopum gebyrað, gyf hwylcum hwæt eglige swyðe, þe he ne betan ne mæge, cyðe hit his geferum and beon syððan ealle georne ymbe þa bote and na ne geswican, ær hi hit gebetan (*Polity*, p. 214, *Incipit de Synodo* 11). It seems from *Canons* 3–6 that the type of synod Wulfstan had in mind was a diocesan gathering of secular clergy under the direction of the bishop, who would inquire into abuses and direct policy towards colleagues and laity and expound procedure for services. It is possible that a document like the *Canons*, or one of the *Pastoral Letters*, would be read out to the gathering. Ælfric writes of his letter to Wulfsige: Nos uero scriptitamus hanc epistolam, quę anglice sequitur, quasi ex tuo ore dictata sit et locutus esses ad clericos tibi subditos ... (*Hirtenbriefe*, p. 1). A relevant passage from Wulfstan occurs at the beginning of the D version of Homily XIII: Wulfstan arcebisceop greteð freondlice þegnas on ðeode, gehadode 7 læwede, ealle

gemænelice þa ðe him betæhte sindon for gode to wissianne. And ic bidde eow for Godes lufan þæt ge þises gewrites giman 7 on hwiltidum hit on gemynde habban . . . (text from *Homilies*, p. 225).

7. Cf. *Conc. Chalced.* IX (quoted from Jost, *Polity*, p. 181): Si clericus adversum clericum habeat negotium, non relinquat suum episcopum et ad saecularia judicia concurrat, sed prius negotium agitetur apud proprium episcopum, vel certe, si fuerit judicium ipsius episcopi, apud arbitros ex utraque parte electos audiatur negotium. Cf. *Incipit de Synodo* 10 (*Polity*, p. 214): na sceotan na to læwedum mannum. The penalty for the offence is given in *Northumbrian Priests' Law*, 5: Gif preost dom to læwedum sceote, þe he to gehadedum scolde, gilde xx or.

gif man þæt nyde scule: Cf. II *Pol.* 17: (cyðe hit man þam cyninge) gif man þæt nyde scyle . . .

8. The best parallel to 8 as a whole is Ælfric 2, 194–5:

> Non licet clerico dimittere ęcclesiam suam, ad quam ordinatus est, et migrare ad alteram, sine permissu episcopi sui.
>
> Quia ęcclesia est eius uxor spiritaliter, per quam spiritales filios generare debet.

Ælfric II, 207 may be dismissed as the immediate source, as it omits the idea of the church as the priest's spiritual wife: Ne sceal nan preost his cyricean forlætan, þe he to ge-hadod bið and to oþere faran, buton his bisceop lyfe for sumon ge-sceade.

rihtæwe: Cf. Homily Xa, 12–13: ac healdan heora riht æwe [*sic*], þæt is heora mynster. Cf. I *Pol.* 77 (II. 153): cirice is sacerdos æwe.

X8 marginal addition **þa hwile þe his lif sig**: this could come from Ælfric I, 73, which is found in X and Cambridge Gg. III. 28 only: Ne nan preost ne fare for ænigre gitsunge fram mynstre to oðrum, ac æfre þurhwunige þær he to gehadod wæs, þa hwyle þe his dagas beoð. Ælfric's source, *Excerptiones pseudo-Ecgberti* XIII, has the phrase *usque ad vitae . . . exitum*. Leo, *Homilia* 679, has a reading very similar to Ælfric and pseudo-Ecgbert, but there is no phrase parallel to X's *þa hwile þe his lif sig*.

Another parallel to the section as a whole is provided by *NPL* 28: Gif preost silfwilles þa circan forlæte, ðe he to gehadod wæs, gebete þæt.

9. Probably from Theodulf, *Capitula* XIV, in view of the fact that *Canons* 10 appears to come from the next section of the *Capitula*, XV: Nullus presbyter fidelibus sanctae Dei Ecclesiae de alterius presbyteri parochia persuadeat, ut ad suam ecclesiam concurrant . . . et suas decimas sibi dent. Cf. Leo, *Homilia* 679: Nullus per pecuniam ecclesiae alterius supplantet. . . . Nullus alterius parochianum . . . ad Missam recipiat. The addition to the source of *gildscipe* is interesting. The Northumbrian priests are believed to have organized themselves into a guild, and the insistence in the early part of the present text on respect for the rights of fellow priests might appear to imply a similar mutually protective organization.

10. From Theodulf, *Capitula* XV: Hoc . . . prohibemus, ut nullus vestrum alterius clericum sollicitet aut recipiat.

COMMENTARY

buton ... folgode: Cf. *Exc. pseudo-Ecgberti* LXI: Si quis alicujus episcopi clericum vel monachum susceperit, *absque consensu illius*, sacrilegus judicetur, et a communione suspendetur ... (my italics).

11. Both Theodulf, *Capitula* III and *Excerptiones pseudo-Ecgberti* XCLI advise manual work for priests, but the latter is nearer to *Can*. 11 in its phrasing: Omnes clerici, qui ad operandum sunt validi, et artificiola et litteras discant. *Capitula* III: *Quod lectioni succedere debeat operatio*. Sed et si quando a lectione cessatur, debet manuum operatio subsequi, quia otiositas inimica est animae.

Wulfstan had voiced the same opinion earlier, in Homily Xa (51–4): Ne beo æfre ænig canonic life þæt sundercræfta sumne ne cunne, ac began georne mynsterlice cræftas 7 geearnian mid þam þæs ðe hig big beon 7 eac æt Gode sylfum ece mede. The practice of such distinguished ecclesiastics as Abbot Ceolfrid, Dunstan, and Athelwold provided notable English examples for this precept.

12. Cf. Homily Xa, 45–6: Ne forseon ða gelæredan na ða ungelæredan, ac læran hi georne ... Jost pointed out ('Einige Wulfstantexte', p. 291) that *Can*. 12 *samlæredan* is a better translation of Amalarius' *minus doctis* than is Xa, 46 *ungelæredan* (although, one might add, it is still not a very close translation); he argued that the compiler of the *Canons* went back to the Latin to make a superior translation. The word *samlæredne* also occurs in the text *Be gehadedum mannum* (sect. 16, p. 221) referred to above under *Can*. 3.

Ælfric III, 190, makes the same point as Xa, in rather different words: Lufiað eow betweonan and gyf hwa lare ne cunne, he leornige æt oðrum, þe gelæred [-ra X] si [and se X] mid eadmodnysse hine gewissige.

gebete hine gif he bet cunne: this is an example of the near-pun noted by Professor Bethurum (*Homilies*, p. 28) in the homilies: two words of the same root but different meaning or part of speech are placed in juxtaposition. The result is an ironical effect typical of Wulfstan. Her examples are: Godes gerihta mid rihte gelæste; fela ungelimpa gelimpð. (Both from *Sermo Lupi*.)

13. From Xa, 46–7: ne ða æþelborenan ne lean þa læsborenan. There is no verbal similarity between *Can*. 13 and the corresponding passage in Amalarius.

14. Without question from Ælfric I, 77: Ne preost ne beo mangere ne gitsigende massere. See Jost, 'Einige Wulfstantexte', p. 296, on this section. He argues most convincingly that the additions to Ælfric I, 77 are typical of Wulfstan's revisions of Ælfric, and compares the versions of the corresponding passage II, 185 in C.C.C.C. 190 (O) and C.C.C.C. 201 (D), of which the latter is usually acknowledged to be a revision by Wulfstan of Ælfric II:

O: Ne mot nan preost beon mangere oþþe gerefa.
D: And witað eac þæt ne mot mid rihte nan preost beon gitsiende mangere ne world-strutere[1] on gerefscire.

---
[1] Word used only by Wulfstan.

Ælfric 2, 171–2 is a further parallel:
Non licet clerico esse mercatorem, nec habere praefecturam.
Nec turpe lucrum sectari nec implicare se negotiis saecularibus.

15. The necessity for the early baptism of children is often stressed, but few texts set a time limit. Ælfric I, 71 is typical: And gif ungefullod cild færlice bið ȝebroht to þam mæssepreost, þæt he hit mot fullian sona mid ofste, þæt hit ne swelte hæðen. Cf. Ælfric II, 177, *Exc. pseudo-Ecgberti* XI.
There is considerable discrepancy between those texts which specify the period within which infants must be baptized. Two compilations from Wulfstan printed by Napier specify a maximum period of 30 days (Napier XXIX, 120/9; LVIII, 300/17), as does Ine 2 (*Gesetze* I, 90). *NPL* 10 specifies nine days. Ælfric 2, 163 agrees with the reading in *Can.* X15, 7 days, which may be preferred to D 37 days: (unusquisque . . . sit sollicitus) In baptizando infantes, ut non sint pagani ultra septem dies. The reading *xxx.vii* may best be explained as a scribal error combining an original *xxx* with a correction to *vii* based on Ælfric. Professor Whitelock has suggested to me that the difference in time limit (30 days as against 7 or 9) may be related to relative density of population: that a priest with a scattered parish might find difficulty in meeting a requirement of 7 days; but although this view would explain Ælfric's 7 days for the relatively densely populated Wessex, it hardly agrees with *NPL*'s 9 for the north. Perhaps the difference is chronologically, not geographically, conditioned.

16. On the implications of the differences between D and X, see above, p. xvii.
No exact source need be cited for this detailed denunciation of pagan practices, for the content is familiar in Wulfstan's works. His repeated condemnations indicate his alarm at what may have been a desperate revival of paganism under the stress of the Danish invasions. Except in Homily XII, *De Falsis Deis*, he is not concerned with organized and formulated paganism, but with witchcraft and superstition, especially the worship of natural objects. The offering of gifts, or making of vows, at trees, wells, or rocks, is frequently condemned, and it would seem that this was the most prevalent form of superstition. The following passages from the homilies offer parallels:

> VI, 85–7: gehatað hy ælmessan þurh deofles lare, oððon to wylle oððon to stane oððon elles to sumum unalyfedum ðingum . . .
>
> VIIIc, 165–8: and ne gyman ge galdra ne idelra hwata, ne wigelunga ne wiccecræfta; 7 ne weorðian ge wyllas ne ænige wudutreowu, forðam æghwylce idele syndon deofles gedwimeru.
>
> Xc, 105–6. Ne ænig man wiccecræft æfre begange. Ne ænig man idola weorðie æfre.
>
> Cf. V Atr. 1, 34; VI Atr. 1, 6; VIII Atr. 44; IX Atr. 1; X Atr. 1; II Cn. 5, 1; *NPL* 54, 54, 1: Gif friðgeard sy on hwæs lande abuton stan oððe treow oððe wille oððe swilces ænigge fleard, þonne gilde se ðe hit worhte lahsliht, healf Criste healf landrican.
>
> 7 gif se landrica nelle to steore filstan, þonne habbe Crist 7 cyningc þa bote.

The precision with which the penalties are specified is surely evidence that pagan practices were a serious problem in the eyes of ecclesiastics. Relevant passages from Wulfstan's habitual sources include *Pen. pseudo-Ecgbert* II, 22–3, IV, 15–16; *Pen. pseudo-Theodore* XXVII, 18: Si quis ad arbores, vel ad fontes, vel ad lapides, sive ad cancellos ... votum voverit ... poeniteat. Passages from other texts of the period are usefully collected in F. Grendon, *Anglo-Saxon Charms*, pp. 140–3.

cristendom ... adwæsce: Cf. *Incipit de Synodo* 3 (*Polity*, p. 211): Bisceopum gebyreð ... þæt hi smeagan ... hu hi cristendom magan fyrmest aræran and [h]æþendom swyðost afyllan. Cf. I *Polity* 116 (II, 221, 235): ænne cristendom georne healdan and ælcne hæðendom mid ealle awurpan.

licwiglunga: Cf. *Can.* 68: and ne geþafige ænig unnitt æt þam lice. The word may be translated 'necromancy': pagan activities associated with a corpse.

hwata and galdra: these, auguries and incantations respectively, are distinguished in VIIIc, 165; see D. Bethurum, *Homilies*, p. 319 n. X's gloss *omen* to *hwata* is interesting: is it a reference to current practice, or merely a little gratuitous classicism?

friðsplottum = *NPL* friðgeard? Evidently a place intended especially for ritual use.

mistlicum ... mistlicum ... mistlicum: for another instance of the repetition of this word in a derogatory context, see *Sermo Lupi* 143, 145.

X16 **þær man ... tihð**: this obscure reference occurs almost verbatim in one of Wulfstan's sources, *Pen. pseudo-Ecgbert* IV, 16: Wif⟨man⟩ beo þæs ylcan wyrðe, gif heo tilað hire cilde mid ænigum wiccecræft oððe æt wega gelætan purh [*sic*] þa eorðan tyhð; forðam (þæt) is mycel hæðenscipe. Raith cites Ælfric, *Lives* XVII, 148–50: Eac sume gewitlease wif farað to wega gelætum 7 teoð heora cild þurh ða eorðan, 7 swa deofle betæcað hi sylfe 7 heora bearn. The process is explained by *Pen. pseudo-Theodore* XXVII, 16: Si quis, pro sanitate filioli, per foramen terrae exierit, illudque spinis post se concludit, XL dies ... poeniteat. A sick child is dragged through a hole in the earth, presumably a pit or trench; his sickness is transferred to the earth, and contained in the hole by stopping it. Grendon (op. cit., p. 130) gives a number of ancient and modern examples of this practice, and later (p. 143) quotes a passage from St. Eligius which further illustrates it: 'Let no one presume ... to make flocks pass through a hollow tree, or an aperture in the earth ...'

wyllweorðunga ... and treowwurðunga and stanwurðunga: Grendon states that these are references to the translocation of diseases; this is not necessarily so, as springs, stones, and trees are the natural objects most commonly associated with animistic practices.

17. A commonplace in Ælfric and Wulfstan; compare *Can.* 22. Two passages from the homilies which may be more relevant to 17 than to 22 are:

> Pater noster 7 credan mymerian þa yldran 7 tæcan heora gingran mid rihtan geleafan (Xc, 170–1).

COMMENTARY

And æfre swa þæt cild raðost ænig ðing specan mæge, tæce man him sona ealra þinga ærest pater noster 7 credan . . . (VIIIc, 142–3).

The former is closely connected with the composition of the *Canons*, probably being written immediately before our text; the latter is usually dated after the *Canons*. For further parallels on instruction in the Creed and Lord's Prayer, see notes to *Can.* 22, where the relation to the sources is of greater interest.

18. From *Pen. pseudo-Theodore* XXXVIII, 9: [Die Dominico] jocationes . . . vel cantica turpia et luxuriosa, vel lusa diabolica, nec ad ipsas aecclesias . . . nec in ullo loco alio facere praesumant.

X18 marginal addition **æt cyrcan**: in view of the phrase *ad ipsas aecclesias* in the source, I suggest that this is a revision by a scribe who referred to the source.

19. From *Pen. pseudo-Theodore* XXXVIII, 8: Opera vero servilia diebus Dominicis nullo modo agantur; id est . . . nec ad placita conveniant . . . D's *folcgemota*, absent from X, agrees with *placita*. Note the difference between *opera servilia* and *cypinge*: one must assume that the author thought the prohibition of labour on Sundays was too well established to need mentioning.

For passages derived from *Can.* 19 see V Atr. 13, 1; VI Atr. 22, 1; VI Atr. 44; 1 Cn. 15; *NPL* 55. It may be significant for differentiating the D and X versions that V and VI Atr. and *NPL* share with D the condemnation of *folcgemota*, whereas I Cn. 15 goes in the direction of X by adding a permissive *butan hit for micelre neodþearfe sig*.

20. From *Exc. pseudo-Ecgberti* CLII, CLIV:

Si quis catholicus capillos totonderit more barbarorum, ab aecclesia Dei alienus habeatur . . .

. . . vir, si utetur veste muliebri, excommunicetur . . .

Ælfric I, 114–15; 2, 175, 193; II, 206, forbid the wearing of women's or lay garments, but say nothing about the hair or beard. The addition of *oððe unefesunge* in X looks like a pedantic gesture by someone who thought that long hair and beard were not implied in *bysmorlicra efesunge*. *Can.* 47 is more explicit.

The reference to garments in the sources makes X *wæda* a better reading than D *ræda*.

21. Cf. *Pen. pseudo-Ecgbert* II, 9: Se man ðe riht-æwe hæfð 7 eac cyfese, ne sylle him nan preost husl ne nan gerihto þe man cristenum mannum deð, butan he to bote gecyrre; 7 gif he cyfesan hæbbe 7 nane riht-æwe, he ⟨ah⟩ ðæs to donne swa him geðincð; wite he þeah þæt he beo on anre gehealdan, beo hit cyfes beo hit æwe. I *Pol.* 75 (II, 151): Læwedum men is ælc wif forboden, buton his rihtæwe . . .

On the argument for the authenticity of this section, see p. xviii, n. 1. Is the dropping of 21 in X in any way connected with the extraordinarily tolerant *NPL* 35? Gif preost cwenan forlæte 7 oðre nime, anathema sit!

22. There can be no doubt that this is derived from Theodulf, *Capitula* XXII (*PL* cv. 198) rather than Ælfric I, 62, or Leo, *Homilia* 681, or *Exc.*

COMMENTARY

pseudo-Ecgberti VI, all of which exhort the priest to make sure that his congregation know the Creed and Lord's Prayer. (Cf. Homily Xc, 170-1.) Moreover, it seems probable that Wulfstan consulted the OE. translation of the *Capitula* at this point, as *Can.* 22 *he ne bið wel cristen* recalls *ne mæg he beon wel cristen* of the OE. *Capitula*. Both Latin and OE. are here given for comparison:

Commonendi sunt fideles ut generaliter omnes, a minimo usque ad maximum, orationem Dominicam et symbolum discant; et dicendum eis, quod in his duabus sententiis omne fidei Christianae fundamentum incumbit, et nisi quis has duas sententias et memoriter tenuerit, et ex toto corde crediderit, et in oratione saepissime frequentaverit, catholicus esse non poterit. Constitutum namque est ut nullus chrismetur, neque baptizetur, neque a lavacro fontis illius suscipiatur, neque coram episcopo ad confirmandum quemlibet teneat, nisi symbolum et orationem Dominicam memoriter tenuerit, exceptis his quos ad loquendum aetas minime perduxit (*PL* cv. 198).

Ealle ge geleaffulle men synt to myngienne gemænlice. from þon læston oð þone mæstan. þ[æt] ælc mon geleornige Pater noster 7 Credan. 7 him is to cyðenne 7 to bodienne. þ[æt] on þissum twam cwydum is se staðol ealles cristenes geleafan. 7 butan hwa þas twegen cwydas asingan mæge. 7 swa gelyfe swa ðær-on sægð. 7 hyne mid oft gebidde. ne mæg he beon wel cristen. Hit wæs gefyrn gesett þ[æt] nan þara manna þe ne cuðe Credan 7 Pater noster þ[æt] he ne moste naþer ne æt biscopes handa ne æt fulwihte nanum men onfoon. ne hine mon furðon fulluhte fullian ne moste. ne biscopian. buton he þa ylde næfde þ[æt] he þonne gyt þa ær genemnedan cwydas geleornian ne mihte (*Ancient Laws*, pp. 477-8).

Homily VIIIc borrows from *Can.* 22 in 148-52: . . . he ne bið wel cristen þe þæt geleornian nele, ne he nah mid rihte æniges mannes æt fulluhte to onfonne, ne æt bisceopes handa se ðe þæt ne cann, ær he hit geleornige, ne he rihtlice ne bið husles wyrðe ne clænes legeres, se ðe on life þæt geleornian nele . . .

VII, 171 echoes the phrase, quite out of context: Se byð wel cristen þe þis [the Commandments] gehealdeð . . . Professor Bethurum comments on this (*Homilies*, p. 311): '*Ðis* may refer to the Creed rather than to the commandment just quoted. Theodulf's sentence in the *Capitula* is the origin of this statement: [quotes from Latin *Capitula*]. See Canons of Edgar 22 and Jost 'Einige Wulfstantexte' pp. 292-3.' If *þis* refers to the Creed, it offers an example of extreme separation of a pronoun from its antecedent. It occurs in one of Wulfstan's characteristic summing-up sentences, and therefore is likely to refer either to the whole content of the homily, or to the content of the immediately preceding sentence. This is not a trivial point, as a reference to the Creed is necessary to establish that the whole phrase is derived from the Latin *Capitula*. Neither Professor Bethurum nor Jost connects the phrase with the OE. *Capitula*, although Jost mentions the existence of the OE. translation ('Einige Wulfstantexte', p. 293). There is clearly some connection, although this is a matter of half-remembering a striking phrase rather than a specific act of copying from a source. None of the inferences which could be drawn from these

parallels can be properly substantiated:
- (a) VIIIc and *Can.* 22 are nearer to OE. *Capitula* than is VII; the borrowing is secondary and therefore VII was written after VIIIc and *Can.* 22.
- (b) Wulfstan knew OE. *Capitula* before VII, half-remembered the phrase when writing VII, but referred directly to OE. *Capitula* when (later) writing *Canons.*
- (c) This is mere coincidence.

23. From *Capitula* XLII: In his jejuniorum diebus nullae lites, nullae contentiones esse debent . . . (*PL* cv. 205). The OE. translation uses the same word as *Can.* 23, *geflyt.*

24. No direct source for this is evident, but Wulfstan thought it important enough to be repeated in V Atr. 18; cf. Ed. Guð. 9. Liebermann, under Gerichtsferien 4a (*Gesetze* II, 463), mentions a Frankish capitulary of 813 which forbids courts on Sundays and Fridays.

25. Both Theodulf and Leo make this recommendation, and Wulfstan repeats it in I *Pol.* 92 (II *Pol.* 197). *Capitula* XLIII is the probable source, as XLII has just been used in *Can.* 23: Abstinendum est enim in his sacratissimis diebus a conjugibus . . . The wording of the OE. *Capitula* is quite unlike that of *Can.* 25. Leo is possible, but is no nearer to *Can.* 25 than is Theodulf: Certis diebus et temporibus conjugatos abstinare ab uxoribus exhortamini (*PL* cxv. 681). Cf. I *Pol.* 92: Nagan læwede men freolstidum ne fæstentidum þurh hæmedþingc wifes gemanan . . .

26. And . . . þeowdome: from Ælfric I, 48: Nu gebyrað mæssepreostum and eallum Godes þeowum, þæt hi healdan heora cyrcan mid halgum þeowdome. The change from *mid halȝum þeowdome* to *mid ealre arwurðnesse to godcundre þenunge and to clænum þeowdome* is an expansion of the type we would expect from Wulfstan. Ælfric's original phrase is rendered by two: *to godcundre þenunge and to clænum þeowdome*; this is preceded by an independent additional adverbial phrase of a type common in the homilies: *mid ealre arwurðnesse.*

The sources of the rest of *Can.* 26 are much more difficult to disentangle. *Capitula* X gives general directions on behaviour in churches:

> Non debetis ad ecclesiam ob aliam causam convenire, nisi ad laudem Domini et ejus servitium faciendum.
> Disceptationes vero, et tumultus, et vaniloquia, et caeterae actiones ab eodem sancto loco penitus prohibendae sunt (*PL* cv. 194).

OE. *Capitula* translates *vaniloquia et caeterae actiones* as *unnytta word. ge gehwylce unnyttnesse*; *Can.* 26 uses *unnit* twice and refers to *idele spæce.* It can be said with some confidence that Wulfstan had this passage from *Capitula* X, perhaps even OE. *Capitula*, in mind, especially as he used *Capitula* IX a little later, in *Can.* 29. But there are also parts of Ælfric's *Pastoral Letters* which correspond fairly well:

> Cristene men sculon secan cyrican gelome, and man ne mot spellian ne spræca drifan binnan Godes cyrican . . .

Ne man ne sceal drincan oððe dollice etan binnan Godes huse ... (I, 105, 106).

Ne man ne mot drincan ne dwollice plegan, ne etan innan cyrican, ne unnytte word þærinne sprecan; ac hine gebiddan (III, 20; cf. 3, 24–5).

The Ælfric passages support D's *gedrync* as against X's *gedryh*.

hund: Jost (*Polity*, p. 188) cites *Admonitio Generalis* 789, no. 71: ... unusquisque vestrum [sc. sacerdotum] videat..., ut ecclesia Dei suam habeat honorem ... et non sit domus Dei et altaria sacrata pervia canibus ...; et ut secularia negotia vel vaniloquia in ecclesiis non agantur.

X hors: this extra item, not in the source, appears intrusive, especially rhythmically; but William of Malmesbury mentions the prohibition of horses from the graveyard, as a sign of respect for the dead (*Vita Wulfstani*, ed. R. R. Darlington, London, 1928, p. 53).

27. The ultimate source of this appears to be *Exc. pseudo-Ecgberti* XXXV: Non oportet aliquid ponere in aecclesia, nisi quae ad ministeria ecclesiastica pertinent ... (*Ancient Laws*, p. 329). Ælfric expands this in 3, 72, and then translates it in III, 115: Mann ne mot na logian and-luman innan cyrican, ne corn ne nan ðing on Cristes huse, buton þam anum þincgum, þe to his þenuncgum gebyriað.

28. From Ælfric I, 107: Nu doð men swa-þeah dyslice for oft, þæt hi willað wacian and wodlice drincan binnan Godes huse and bysmorlice plegian and mid gegaf-spræcum Godes hus gefylan. Cf. 3, 25: Et qui in ęcclesia uigilant, non manducent in ea nec bibant.

29. From *Capitula* IX: Nemo in ecclesia sepeliatur, nisi forte talis sit persona sacerdotis, aut cujuslibet justi hominis, quae per vitae meritum talem vivendo suo corpori defuncto locum acquisivit (*PL* cv. 194).

Ðonne nelle we nu heononforð þ[æt] mon ænigne in cyrcean byrie. butan hit hwylc sacerdhades mon sy. oððe eft swa rihtwis læwede. þ[æt] mon wite þ[æt] he on his lifes geearnunge libbende swilce stowe geearnode his lichoman on to ræstanne (*Ancient Laws*, p. 472).

bute man wite: cf. *þ[æt] mon wite* as a further slight piece of evidence that Wulfstan used the OE. *Capitula*.

30. From Ælfric I, 69–70:

Eac hy gesetton þæt mann ne sceole mæssian innan nanum huse, buton hyt gehalgod sy.
Buton for mycelre neode, oððe ȝyf mann bið untrum.

Other passages from Wulfstan's usual sources give no provision for sickness. They are: Ælfric III, 19; 3, 23; *Exc. pseudo-Ecgberti* IX, LIII; Leo 677; *Capitula* XI. Note that *Capitula* IX, X, and XI are paralleled in practically adjacent sections of the *Canons*, 29, 26, and 30 respectively.

31. From Ælfric 2, 142: Et non debet celebrare missam ... nisi ... super altare sanctificato ...

COMMENTARY

32. Cf. the sources for *Can.* 34. Ælfric lists all the books which would be necessary for a priest's ministry; but he does not specifically forbid a priest to celebrate without the *mæsseboc*.

33. Leo is the only source which lists vestments:

Nullus cantet [sc. missam] . . . sine amictu, sine alba, stola, fanone, et casula. Vestimenta nitida sint . . . (675).
Corporale mundissimum sit (677).

Cf. Ælfric I, 55, 58: He sceal habban eac mæsse-reaf, þæt he mage arwurðlice Gode sylfum þenigan, swa hit gedafenlic is. . . . clæne corporale . . .

2, 140: Et debet habere clara et integra officialia indumenta.

corporale(m): the *Oxford Dictionary of the Christian Church* defines this as: 'a square piece of linen on which the bread and wine are placed and consecrated in the Eucharist. Such a cloth was used in the fourth century, but there was no distinction between the corporal and the ordinary linen altar cloth now used under the corporal before the ninth century.'

D **subumlem**, X **subumbrale**: Du Cange records **subumla** but the word could be (1) *subarmale*—but this was usually a military term. (2) *subu(n)cula* = *colobium*, a short-sleeved or sleeveless undergarment; this is perhaps the form behind *subumlem*: cf. *Can.* 46 and note. (3) The most plausible explanation is that *subumbrale* = *superhumerale*. This was a term for *amictus* (now *amice*), described by the *Oxford Dictionary of the Christian Church* as: 'A linen cloth, square or oblong in shape, with strings attached. In the W. Church it is worn round the neck by the priest when celebrating the Eucharist, and by other ministers who wear the alb.' The *amictus* was, as Wulfstan says, worn under the alb. (But see McAlister, *Ecclesiastical Vestments*, who defines *superhumerale* as 'alb'). The acceptance of *subumbrale* = *superhumerale* = *amictus* is made easier by the mention of *amictus* by Leo. Jost (*Polity*, p. 190) notes: 'Hs. *subumlem*, nach X für *subumbralem*, d.h. *sub[h]umeralem*; das zweite *b* ist Gleitelaut zwischen *m* und *r*. Ich vermag *subhumerale* bzw. *subhumeralis* nicht zu belegen. Doch ist es offenbar = *humerale* [refers to *amictu* in Leo], und das *sub*- soll bloß verdeutlichen, daß es unter der Albe getragen wird.'

alba: *Oxford Dictionary of the Christian Church*: 'A white linen garment, reaching from the neck to the ankles and held at the waist by a girdle, worn by the ministers at Mass.'

34. From Ælfric I, 52–4, where the *gode . . . becc* are specified:

He sceal habban eac þa wæpna to þam gastlicum weorce, ær-þan-þe he beo gehadod, þæt synd þa halgan bec: saltere and pistolboc, godspellboc and mæsseboc, sangboc and handboc, gerim and pastoralem, penitentialem and rædingboc.

þas bec sceal mæssepreost nede habban, and he ne mæg butan beon, gif he his had on riht healdan wyle and þam folce æfter rihte wisigan, þe him to-locað.

And beo he æt þam wær, þæt hi beon wel gerihte.

This is repeated with variations in Ælfric 2, 137–9 and II, 157–8, which also includes the phrase *wel gerihte* which is echoed in *Can.* 34.

COMMENTARY 33

35. This regulation appears in Theodulf, *Capitula* VII, Leo, *Homilia* 675 and 678, and Ælfric III, 84. Of these Ælfric gives the version which is closest to *Can*. 35: Ne most þu na ana mæssian, butan man ðe andwyrde. Leo makes the same point twice:

> Nullus missam cantet solus . . .
> Omnis presbyter clericum habeat scholarem, qui . . . ad missam respondeat . . .

The Latin *Capitula* is longer and more diffuse than Leo or Ælfric, but the OE. translation of this passage is a free one which agrees better than the Latin with *Can*. 35, and is in one detail closer than Ælfric: OE. *Capitula oncwæðe* agrees with *Can*. *acweðe* against Ælfric *andwyrde*: Ne sculon mæsse-preostas nates-hwon nænig þinga ænlipie butan oðrum mannum mæssan syngan. þ[æt] he wite hwone he grete. 7 hwa him oncwæðe (*Ancient Laws*, p. 472).

D **næbbe**: X **hæbbe**. I have inserted a semi-colon in X to make *hæbbe* more acceptable, but the word is probably a mistake.

36. Cf. Theodulf, *Additio ad Capitulare* (*PL* cv. 208): et nulli extra parvulos et infirmos . . . edere et bibere praesumant ante publicum peractum officium. Neither *Pen. pseudo-Theodore* XXXIX, 12 nor Leo makes any allowance for the sick:

> Qui acceperit sacrificium post cybum, vii. dies poeniteat (*Ancient Laws*, p. 299).
> Nullus cantet [sc. missam] nisi jejunus (*Homilia*, *PL* cxv. 675).

37. **þrywa**: Jost, *Polity*, p. 191, cites *Conc. Triburiense* 875 Ch. II, p. 224, 2: Nihilominus statuimus et iudicamus nulli sacerdoti esse licitum una die uno altare plus quam tres superponere missas. Ælfric II, 75 and 3, 73, both derived from *Exc. pseudo-Ecgberti* LV, forbid the celebration of mass more than once in a day; but 3, 75 allows a second if necessary: Quidam tamen pro defunctis unam faciunt et alteram de die, si necesse est. This agrees with the alteration of *þriwa* in X to *twiga*. The alteration appears to be in the same neat hand which modified 18, 20, and 41 in X (hand 4).

38. Both Ælfric and the main penitentials insist on the greatest care being taken of the consecrated bread and wine; Ælfric's argument is that, although the bread and wine must always be kept ready for dying men, they must not be neglected, and must be replaced every week or fortnight. He condemns the practice of consecrating the bread and wine at Easter and keeping them throughout the year in the belief that they are more holy than if they were consecrated at any other time.

Can. 38 seems to have been suggested by Ælfric I, 133-6:

> Sume preostas healdað þæt husl, þe bið on easterdæg gehalgod, ofer gear to seocum mannum.
> Ac hi misdoð swiðe deope, þæt þæt husl sceole fynegian, and nellað understandan, hu mycele dædbote seo penitentialis tæcð be þam, gyf þæt husel bið fynig oððe hæwen, oððe gif hit forloren bið, oððe gif mys þurh gymeleaste hit etað.

Man sceal healdan þæt halige husl mid mycelre gyminge, and ne forhealdan hit.

Ac halgian oðer edniwe to seocum mannum, a embe seofon niht oððe ymbe feowertyne, þæt hit huru fynig ne sy.

And we læraŏ ... þearf sy: *Exc. pseudo-Ecgberti* XXII: Ut presbiter eucharistiam habeat semper paratam ad infirmos ...
and þa axsan ... forgimde: *Pen. pseudo-Theodore* XXXIX, 5: Qui neglexerit sacrificium ... poeniteat, et in igne projiciatur, cynisque ejus sub altare abscondatur ... For the section as a whole, cf. also Theodulf, *Capitula* V and *Can.* 43.

39. From *Exc. pseudo-Ecgberti* C: Sacerdotes Dei diligenter semper procurent, ut panis et vinum, et aqua, sine quibus nequaquam missae celebrantur, pura et munda fiant; quia si aliter agatur, cum his qui acetum cum felle mixtum Domino optulerunt, nisi vera penitentia subvenerit, punientur.

7 wa þam ... todeð: cf. Theodulf, *Capitula* V: et nihil in his vile, nihil non probatum inveniatur. ...

X forðam he deð: omitted in D as a result of the repetition of *deð*.

clæne oflete: cf. Ælfric 3, 32: Debet namque sacerdos dei sollicite curare, ut oblatio eius munda sit et non uetusta. Cf. also Ælfric 2, 140; II, 159; III, 70, 74.

38-9 reappear in *De ecclesiasticis gradibus* 37-9 (*Polity*, p. 237). This piece occurs in D, X, and C.C.C.C. 190, and Jost's text is taken from X:

... georne sculon hyg gyman, þæt ða þing, þe to ðam husle gebyriað, clænlice behworfene beon, þæt is hlaf and win and wæter.

Ne mæg ænig mæsse beon gemæssod butan þam þreom þingum; gyf hwa elles deð, wa him ðære dæde!

And gyf þa þing mishworfene bið, þonne byð þæt gelic þam, swylce man geefenlæce þam, þe eced and geallan mencgdon tosomne and on bysmor hit syððan Criste gebudon.

40. From Ælfric 3, 68 and 71, or 2a, XI-XII:

Presbyter missam celebrans et non audens sumere sacrificium, accusante conscientia sua, anathema est. (Cf. *Can.* 68e, mæssige gyf he durre.)

Qui bis sacrificium unum consecrat, similis est illi qui unum infantem bis baptizat, et uterque anathema est.

This is quoted and paraphrased in III, 93-4 and 97:

Sume preostas nellað þicgan þæt husel, þe hyg halgiað. Nu willað we eow secgan, hu seo boc segð be þam:

Presbiter missam ... Se mæssepreost, þe mæssað and ne dear ðæt husel ðicgan, wat hine scildigne, se is amansumad. [cp. gloss on X41]

Se-ðe tuwa halgað ane ofletan to husle, se bið ðam gedwolan gelic, þe an cyld fulað tuwa.

These sources shed light on the phrase *ne nænne man fullige oftor þonne æne* which is added to 41 in X only: it seems that the additional material is authentic, but that it should follow *Can.* 40, not 41.

COMMENTARY

Cf. Leo 675: Nullus cantet qui non communicet.

gehalgod: with the omission after this word, cf. that after *gehaldogan/-um* in D and X 22.

41. Ælfric specifies the materials of which a chalice may be made in I, 58; 2, 141; II, 161–2. II is the only one of the *Pastoral Letters* which forbids the use of a wooden chalice, and this addition may have been made under Wulfstan's influence.

> Beo his calic geworht of ecum[1] antimbre, gylden oþþe sylfren, glæsen oþþe tinen.
> Ne beo he na hyrnen, ne huru treowen.

X 41 **Gylden oððe seolfren tinen**, added carefully in the margin, could come from any of the Ælfric parallels. Note that all list glass as well as gold, tin, and silver; but these materials are listed in different orders:

> gylden oððe seolfern [*sic*] oþþe tinen oð glæsen ... (I, 58 [X]).
> de auro, uel de argento siue stagno uel uitro (2, 141).
> gylden oþþe sylfren, glæsen oþþe tinen (II, 161).

It may be hazardous to suggest that the annotator would be more likely to omit a unit from the end of the list (i.e. in I or 2) than from the middle (i.e. in II). If the annotator was referring to the same manuscript, X, he would have access to Ælfric I only; moreover, the other version of Ælfric I (C.C.C.C. 190) omits the phrase entirely. I would suggest that this is the hand of a scribe engaged in correcting this version of the *Canons* by reference to the sources within the same manuscript, sometimes making it more specific, sometimes bringing the work up to date. His hand (4) appears in *Canons* 18, 20, 37, and 41.

42. This partly repeats material given in 26 and 27.

and a sy byrnende ... singe: from Leo, Homilia 675: Nullus cantet sine lumine. Ælfric I, 33 and II, 104 define the duties of the acolyte as the carrying of a candle at mass; it is taken for granted that a light will be used: Acolitus is gecweden seþe [*sic*] candele oððe tapor byrð to Godes þenungum, þonne mann godspell ræt oððe þonne man halgað þæt husl æt þam weofode (I, 33).

43. Cf. notes to 38. Theodulf, *Capitula* V (*PL* cv. 193) is closer to 43 than to 38, especially as it specifies the various parts of the Eucharist which are to be looked after: diligenter observetur ut panis, et vinum, et aqua, sine quibus missae nequeunt celebrari, mundissime atque studiose tractentur ... The closeness of the material in 43 to that in 38 and 39 is emphasized by X's repetition of lines and phrases from these sections. *gehalgod oft* recalls *clæne oflete* in 39, and the last part of X43 recalls X38. I have followed Thorpe's suggestion that X *of(e)t* is a corruption of *oflet*, although he is influenced by the glossator in his translation 'fruits (?)'.

44. From Theodulf, *Capitula* VI, rather than Leo 678 or *Pen. pseudo-Theodore* XLVI, because *Capitula* V is used in the preceding section: Feminae, missam sacerdote celebrante, nequaquam ad altare accedant, sed locis suis stent ... (*PL* cv. 193).

---

[1] D has *myltendum*—cf. *Can.* 41 *gegoten*.

COMMENTARY

45. From Ælfric I, 49–51:

And þa seofon tidsangas gesyngon þærinne, þe him gesette synd, swaswa se sinoð hi gedihte:
Uhtsang and primsang, undernsang and middægsang, nonsang and æfensang and nihtsang seofoðan.
And hi sceolon gebiddan geornlice for þone cyning and for heora bisceop und [*sic*] for þa þe him god doð and for eall cristen folc (cf. *Cn.* 70).
Cf. Ælfric 2, 62–4; II, 69–73.

On rihtne timan: cf. *Exc. pseudo-Ecgbert* II: ... horis competentibus diei et noctis.

46. From *Exc. pseudo-Ecgberti* CLIV: Quicunque clericus visus fuerit in aecclesia sine colobio vel cappa . . . excommunicetur.

D mæssepreosta oððe mynsterpreosta: Bosworth–Toller take *mynsterpreost* to be 'a priest who conducts service in a minster'; but the word *mynster* is ambiguous in OE. Its more frequent meaning is 'monastic church', but a reference to monastic practice is out of place in the *Canons*. We may suspect Wulfstan of tautology for stylistic reasons, as is common with him: cf. *Can.* 14 *mangere . . . massere*.

X gewæpned: the insertion of this word changes the construction of the sentence to make entry into the *weofodsteall* (sanctuary) only, and not the whole church, conditional upon wearing the *oferslop*; this does not agree with *Excerptiones in aecclesia*. Ælfric condemns the wearing of weapons by priests, but says nothing of their wearing weapons in church, because this is implied in the general statement: Ne mot he wæpnu werian ne to ge-feohte faran (II, 189).

D oferslipe: X **oferslope:** Bosworth–Toller define *oferslype* as an alb or surplice. This raises difficulties, as the alb had wrist-length sleeves, whereas the colobium, which Wulfstan seems to translate here, had no sleeves or very short sleeves. *Oferslop = byrrum* (a cloak) according to Bosworth–Toller *Supplement*, where the word is compared with ON. *yfirsloppr*. Both *oferslop* and *oferslipe* appear to indicate an originally sleeveless garment, distinct from the alb.

D weohstealle: X **weofodstealle:** Bosworth–Toller gives a further instance of *weohsteall*: 'He eode binnan þonne weohstal on norð healfe' from *An Old English Vision of Leofric*, ed. A. S. Napier, *Transactions of the Philological Society*, 1908, p. 68. *Weocsteall* 'absida' also occurs (see *Englische Studien*, xi. 64, 6). But *weofodsteall* < [*weoh*+*beod*]+*steall* is the usual form. Both words are to be found under *wigsteall* in Bosworth–Toller.

47. From *Exc. pseudo-Ecgberti* CLIII–IV: Petrus itaque Apostolus clericali tonsura primo usus est. . . . Quicunque clericus . . . si non more Romano capillos et barbam totonderit, excommunicetur . . . Cf. CLII, quoted in note to *Can.* 20. See also *NPL* 34: Gif preost sceare misgime beardes oððe feaxes, gebete þæt.

48. This presumably refers to uniformity in the reckoning of feast- and fast-days and in informing the congregation of these dates. We are reminded of the old bitter controversy over the date of Easter. The text *Be*

COMMENTARY

gehadedum mannum printed by Jost, *Polity*, pp. 217–22, states that the candidate for ordination must be able to demonstrate *hu he on gerimcræfte gearryne tosceadan cunne* (sect. 13); Ælfric I, 52 requires that a priest should possess a *gerim* among his necessary books. Cf. *Can.* X50.

49. Cf. Theodulf, *Capitula* XXXVIII: Diebus vero jejunii eleemosyna facienda est, et cibum vel potum, quo quisque uti debuit, si non jejunaret, pauperibus eroget . . . (*PL* cv. 204).

50. X *efenforðe* is, in the context provided by 48, a better reading than D *efenweorðe*.

51. From Ælfric III, 80: And ic secge eow to soþan, þæt ge sceolan læran cnapan and geonge men eow to fultume, þæt hig æfter eow don þa ylcan þenunga. Cf. Ælfric 3, 40; *Capitula* XX.

52. From *Exc. pseudo-Ecgberti* III: Ut omnibus festis et diebus Dominicis unusquisque sacerdos Evangelium Christi praedicet populo. Cf. Ælfric I, 61 (cf. 2, 159 and II, 175). *Excerptiones* III is preferred to Ælfric as Wulfstan's source as IV and V are used in the nearby *Can.* 54 and 55–6 respectively.

bodigan and aa wel bisnian: cf. Ælfric I, 42: He sceal þæt folc læran to geleafan mid bodunge and mid clænum þeawum þam cristenum gebysnian. I *Polity* 67: And ægðer hi sculon, ge wel bodian ge wel bisnian . . . and for eal cristen folc geornlice gebiddan.

53. The drinking of blood is forbidden in two of Wulfstan's sources. *Pen. pseudo-Theodore* XXXI, 31: Si quis voluntarie sanguinem animalium, contra praeceptum Domini faciens, comederit, iii. annos poeniteat . . . *Pen. pseudo-Ecgbert* IV, 23: Gif hwa blod ete oððe styrfig flæsc, 7 he hit for neode ne do, fæste . . . IV, 24 elaborates on *styrfig flæsc*, and in one phrase explains the partly illegible addition in D: Gif wulf *æniges cynnes orf* ⟨to⟩ slite 7 hit for þam dead beo, ne abite his nan cristen man . . . The same idea finds expression in Homily Xc: Ne ænig man myrtenes æfre ne abite ne blodes ne abyrige (104–5).

54. **And we . . . oðrum þingum**: from *Exc. pseudo-Ecgberti* IV: Et unusquisque sacerdos cunctos sibi pertinentes erudiat, ut sciant qualiter decimas totius facultatis ecclesiis divinis debite offerant. The difference between the versions of 54 in D and X is of a similar nature to that between D and X 16. Additional material has been inserted in X, and the order of phrases has been altered, to a degree beyond that of scribal tampering. 16 and 54 are among the longest and most developed sections of the *Canons*, and this may indicate their importance in Wulfstan's eyes. Another measure of their importance is the fact that they were used in the laws which Wulfstan compiled after the *Canons*—54 is reproduced in V Atr. 11–11, 1, VI Atr. 16–19, and VIII Atr. 9–12, 1 (*Gesetze* I, 240, 252, and 265). Wulfstan may have spent more than usual effort over the phrasing of these paragraphs, with the result that different versions were perpetuated through being copied separately. It is interesting that X54

COMMENTARY

is closer than D54 to the relevant passage from V Atr., which shares with X the mention of *leohtgescot*:

7 gelæste man Godes gerihta georne æghwylce geare.

Ðæt is sulhælmessan xv niht onufan eastran 7 geogoðe teoðunge be pentecosten 7 eorðwæstma be ealra halgena mæssan 7 Romfeoh be Petres mæssan 7 leohtgescot þriwa on geare (V Atr. 11-11, 1).

Cf. X54 *leohtgesceotu þriwa on geare* ... *Leohtgescot* is also included in the list in Homily XIII (77-8), in Ed. Guð. 6, 2 (*Gesetze* I, 132), and in Napier LXI, where the terms are specified as Christmas, Candlemas, and Easter. The folios of the York Gospels which contain Napier LIX-LXI (158-9^v) have been annotated in the hand which may be Wulfstan's own; Wulfstan would not have let an irregular requirement pass uncorrected, and perhaps we can infer that the version in the York Gospels was designed for the northern province, that in the *Canons* not. I am indebted to Professor Whitelock for this suggestion.

sulhælmessan: a penny for every working plough.

geoguðe teoðunge: a tithe on new-born livestock. No yield had to be made in respect of wild animals on lay territory.

eorðwestma: a tithe on crops, including uncultivated products.

Romfeoh: Peter's Pence.

ciricsceat: an ancient due which was an all-purposes endowment for providing the church with an income.

leohtgesceotu: payment for the provision of candles for the church.

55. As part of 54 is derived from *Exc. pseudo-Ecgberti* IV, and 56 from the latter part of V, we may suggest the first clause of V as the source for 55, although the verbal parallel is not very close: Ut ipsi sacerdotes a populis suscipiant decimas et dividant ...

56. This comes from *Excerptiones* V: ... et ad ornamentum ecclesiae primam eligant partem; secundam autem, ad usum pauperum atque peregrinorum, ... tertiam vero sibimetipsis sacerdotes reservent. Ælfric I, 68 reproduces this: And gange se sacerd to and dæle hy on þreo: ænne dæl to cyricbote and oðerne þearfum, þone þriddan þam Godes þeowum, þe þære cyrcan begymað. The tripartite division should be taken as referring to free charitable donations, not obligatory dues, the subject of 54.

58. From Theodulf, *Capitula* XIII: Observandum vobis est, ut et vos ab ebrietate abstineatis, et ut plebes subditae abstineant praedicetis ... (*PL* cv. 195). Ælfric I, 74; 2, 173; II, 186; Leo, *Homilia* 678, all warn clerics against drunkenness, but say nothing of preaching to the laity against it: in keeping with the purpose of this work, Wulfstan couples the priest's own morality with his care for that of his congregation.

59. Perhaps suggested by the second part of *Capitula* XIII: et neque per tabernas eatis bibendo aut comedendo, neque domos aut vicos curiositate qualibet peragretis, neque cum feminis aut cum quibuslibet impuris personis convivia exerceatis. Nisi forte paterfamilias quilibet vos ad domum suam invitaverit, et cum sua conjuge et prole velit vobiscum spiritali

COMMENTARY 39

gaudio laetari, et verborum vestrorum refectionem accipere, et vobis refectionem carnalem charitatis officio exhibere; oportet enim, ut si quando quilibet fidelium carnalibus vos reficit epulis, a vobis reficiatur epulis spiritalibus. Ælfric III, 188 has the more specific command: Ne ȝe ȝliȝmenn ne beon. Jost (*Polity*, p. 201) cites *Canones Hibernenses* X: Clericus inter epulas cantans, fidem utique non aedificans, sed auribus tantum pruriens, excommunis sit. Note that the *Canones Hibernenses* are found in Hatton 42, and that Wulfstan's knowledge of this MS. is confirmed by the fact that it contains entries in the hand believed to be his own.

Cf. *Incipit de Synodo* 8 (*Polity*, p. 213), which might also be compared with *Can*. 65: Bisceopum gebyreþ, þæt hi ne beon to gliggeorne, ne hunda ne hafeca hedan to swyðe . . .

60. From Ælfric I, 82: Ne he aðas ne swerige, ac mid anfealdnysse sprece æfre unleaslice, swa-swa gelæred Godes þeowa. Cf. Ælfric III, 186; *Exc. pseudo-Ecgberti* XIX.

61 (X68a). Two sentences from Homily Xa provide a close parallel to 61:

Forbugan hi a wifmanna neaweste swa hi æfre geornost magon (33–4). Ne beon hi . . . æwbrecan, ac healdan heora riht æwe, þæt is heora mynster (11–13).

Cf. Ælfric I, 2, 16a; 2, 195; *Excerptiones* XV, which forbids a priest to have any woman living in his house; several passages in the *Pastoral Letters*, derived from this, make the same order, debarring even mother or sister. I *Polity* 72 (II, 148) is more specific than *Can*. 61: Nis nanum weofodþegne alifed, þæt he wifian mote, ac is ælcum forboden. I *Pol*. 75 (II, 151) leaves us in no doubt that marriage was not uncommon among priests. Clerical marriage was thought to be adultery because (I, 77, II, 151) *Cirice is sacerdos æwe*; cf. I, 105 (II, 210). But the variation in practice—or tolerance—in this matter of clerical marriage is illustrated by *NPL* 35, which, far from forbidding sexual relations to priests, forbids only desertion: Gif preost cwenan forlæte 7 oðre nime, anathema sit! We are reminded once again of the difference between the northern and southern areas. Perhaps the omission of 21 in X, and the displacement of 61 to 68a, indicate its compiler's uncertainty on this subject.

62. This is expanded in VIII Atr. 27: Gif mæssepreost ahwar stande on leasre gewitnesse oððe on mænan aðe oððe þeofa gewita 7 geweorhta beo, þonne sy he aworpen of gehadodra gemanan . . .

It will be convenient here to present my reasons for regarding 62 as influencing VIII Atr. 27, but 68b, e–i as later interpolations from VIII Atr. 28–30, 19–24, although it would be simpler to regard the borrowing as operating in the same direction in both cases.

First, VIII Atr. 27 is a rewritten form of Can. 62: it is an expansion, of the type Wulfstan is known to have made, of a short passage in order to bring it into line with his characteristic style. 62 is, like the majority of the sections of the *Canons*, terse and concise. In VIII Atr. 27 the original short sentence has been expanded by the addition of extra phrases so that we are left with Wulfstan's usual two-stress rhythm and his paired phrases: Gif mǽssepreóst / áhwar stánde / on léasre gewítnesse / oððe on mǽnan áðe / oððe þeófa gewíta / 7 gewéorhta béo, / þonne sý he awórpen / of gehádodra gemánan / . . . / It is generally assumed that Wulfstan's stylistic alterations were nearly always expansions of this type, and rarely contractions: therefore the development of this passage is more likely to have been *Can.*→Atr. than vice versa. On the other hand, the relationship between *Can.* 68b, e–i and VIII Atr. 28–30, 19–24 is one of verbatim quotation, with minor variants which could be explained as merely scribal. This situation is rare in Wulfstan: passages which occur in several of his works always involve some degree of rewriting (cf. the parallels to *Can.* 2, 54). Either 68b, e–i or VIII Atr. 19–24, 28–30 must be described as an interpolation by someone other than Wulfstan.

The fact that 62 occurs in both D and X is strongly in favour of its authenticity; conversely, the additions to 68 are in X only, and perhaps this casts doubt on their authenticity.

Finally, the apparent continuity, both in text and sources, of 68 and 69 corroborates the impression that 68a–i are out of context, whereas there is no reason for believing that the parallels in VIII Atr. are out of their proper context.

(Jost cites I Cn. 5–5, 2c for 68 e–i, and in fact these sections sometimes provide closer parallels than VIII Atr. Professor Whitelock suggests that the order may have been VIII Atr. → *Canons* → I Cn. Of course the order D *Canons* → VIII Atr. → X *Canons* → I Cn. is not contradictory to my argument. Unfortunately the material is too extensive to be set out here.)

63. Jost (*Polity*, p. 202) translates this difficult section: 'Und wir verordnen, daß ein Priester niemals ein umstrittenes Ordal durch Eid gültig mache(?)' (And we decree that a priest may never make a disputed ordeal valid by an oath.) He comments: 'Die Übersetzung ist zweifelhaft. Liebermann, Archiv für neuere Sprachen, Bd. 151, 81, deutet *geæðe = geeðe = geieðe* "erleichtern" und übersetzt entsprechend. Daß die beiden von einander unabhängigen Hss. *geæðe* für *geieðe* aufweisen sollten, ist mir aber nicht glaubhaft.' Thorpe translates *Can.* 63 (*Ancient Laws*, p. 401): 'And we enjoin, that a priest engaged in litigation never be juror in an ordeal.' He comments: 'This interpretation is purely conjectural: that "bisæce" may be an adjective, signifying *litigious, disputable*, appears from the only place I have elsewhere met with the word, viz. Const. VII. . . . That the text is corrupt, is rendered less probable from the concurrence of both MSS. which have obviously not been copied from a common source.' Jost's translation seems acceptable, and agrees with the definitions of Bosworth–Toller *Supplement*: ge-æþan 'to make an oath concerning', 'confirm by oath'; *bisæce*: adj. (correcting the earlier interpretation of it as a noun), related to *sacan* 'to fight, contend', here 'disputed', 'in litigation'.

65. First sentence: Jost (*Polity*, p. 202) quotes Ratherii Episc. Veronensis, *Praeloquiorum Libri Sex* V. 6 (*PL* cxxxvi. 291): Qui [Bischöfe] trocho ludant, aleam vero nequaquam fugiunt; qui tabula quam Scriptura, disco exercentur quam libro.

COMMENTARY

Se canon is *Pen. pseudo-Ecgbert* IV, 27, 28, which is quoted almost verbatim as *Can.* 65 (second sentence) and 66.

66-7. 66 is from *Pen. pseudo-Ecgbert* IV, 28, practically verbatim. 67 reappears as part of 69. Its presence here may be explained by two Ælfric parallels which link abstinence with readiness to carry out one's duties:

> Ne nan preost þurh dysig ne drynce ungemetelice, ne nænne mann ne neadige to mycclum drynce.
> Forþan-þe he sceall beon gearo, gif cild bið to fulligenne oððe man to husligenne, þæt he hæbbe his gewitt (I, 74-5).
> Nec esse ebriosum, nec bibere in tabernis.
> Sed oportet eum semper esse paratum ad hoc quod ordinatus est (2, 173-4).

68. This has a complex indebtedness to several passages from Ælfric, and illustrates Wulfstan's thoroughness in consulting several sources before writing a particular section. Both 68 and 69 are longer than most sections and constitute a summary of the duties of the secular priest as they affect his congregation. The similarity of material in 68 and 69, and their summarizing tendencies, suggest that they were designed to go together, to form the conclusion of the work. If this is so, then 68a–i are certainly interpolated.

And ... smerige: from Ælfric I, 83–5:

> He sceal eac mid gesceade þa syngigendan scrifan ælcne be his mæðe, swa-swa he acuman maʒe.
> And he sceal husligan unhale and seoce ...
> ... and smyrigan þa seocan symble on legere.

Ælfric 2, 165–8, repeat the material of I, 83–5, but supply the source for *dædbote tæce* and for the second half of 68:

> In dando poenitentiam peccantibus.
> In uisitando infirmos.
> Et communicando eos et unguendo, si hoc desiderant et confessionem faciant.
> In sepeliendo mortuos et orando pro eis.

and hi eac smerige gif hi þæs girnan: Ælfric II, 178: Gif se seoca man gyrnað, þæt man hine smyrige ...

and æfter forðsiðe ... bebirge: Ælfric 2, 168: In sepeliendo mortuos et orando pro eis. Ælfric II, 181a (D): And gif him forðsið gebirige, bestande man þæt lic wislice and georne þa sawle Gode betæcan.

and ne geþafige ænig unnitt: this is a typical (though not very explicit) condemnation of superstitious practices or merrymaking before the burial of a dead man (perhaps not specifically necromancy, but cf. *Can.* 16). Ælfric I, 112–13 gives more details of the practices which the priest must not tolerate:

> forbeode ge þa hæðenan sangas þæra læwedra manna and heora cheahchetunga.
> Ne ge sylfe ne eton, ne ne drincon, þær þæt lic inne lið, þe-læs-þe ge syndon efenlæce þæs hæðenscypes, þe hy þær begað.

X68a = D61.

68b–i. From VIII Atr. 28–30, 19–24; cf. I Cn. 5–5, 2c; for comments see note to *Can.* 62.

68b. First sentence: cf. first sentence of Bx (above, p. 21) and a text printed by Jost (*Polity*, p. 169) from X f. 20^{rv}: And gyf mæssepreost his agen lif rihtlice fadige, weaxe his wyrðscype.

Second sentence and 68a: cf. I *Polity* 77 (II, 153): Cirice is sacerdos æwe. Nah he mid rihte ænige oðre; forðam ne gebirað sacerdan nan ðingc, naðor ne to wife ne to worldwige, gif hi Gode willað rihtlice hiran and Godes laga healdan . . .

68h. **corsnæde**: A method of ordeal sometimes administered when the accused was an ecclesiastic: a morsel of consecrated bread or cheese was given to the accused when he swore his innocence; if it stuck in his throat, he was deemed guilty. It is not mentioned in the laws outside the two texts of VIII Atr., which the *Canons* are using. Rituals for the conduct of this form of ordeal are printed by Liebermann, *Gesetze* I, pp. 408 ff., 425–7.

69. **ġe fulluhtele ġe seocum smyrels**: from Ælfric I, 85: Se preost sceal habban gehalgodne ele on sundron to cildum and on sundran to seocum mannum . . . This source links 69 with 68.

and cristendom firðriġe: cf. *Can.* 16 *cristendom geornlice arære* and note.

ġe wel bodiġe ġe wel bisniġe: cf. *Can.* 52 *bodigan and aa wel bisnian* and note.

þonne . . . bið: a favourite closing phrase of Wulfstan's; cf. Homily II, 71–2: þonne geleanað he hit us swa us leofast bið; III, 78–9; VIIa, 47–8.

70. A misplaced item, associated by its sources with *Can.* 45. From Ælfric I, 51: And hi sceolon gebiddan geornlice for þone cyninȝ and for heora bisceop, und [*sic*] for þa, þe him god doð and for eall cristen folc.

Cf. *Excerptiones pseudo-Ecgberti* VII–VIII:

Ut cuncti sacerdotes precibus assiduis pro vita et imperio domini imperatoris . . . orent.

Ut unusquisque sacerdos cotidianis assistat orationibus pro pontifice, cujus gubernatur regimine.

On the priest's duty to pray for his bishop, cf. the text *Be gehadedum mannum* 21 (*Polity*, p. 222): aa heora lifdagas gebiddon þærtoeacan for hine [i.e. the bishop] georne.

BIBLIOGRAPHY

1. PRIMARY MATERIAL

(a) Previous editions of the Canons of Edgar

THORPE, B., *Ancient Laws and Institutes of England* (folio edition, London, 1840), pp. 395–402. (Two-volume edition, ii, 244–65.)

JOST, K., *Die 'Institutes of Polity, Civil and Ecclesiastical', ein Werk Erzbischof Wulfstans von York*, Schweizer Anglistische Arbeiten, xliii (Bern, 1959), 178–209.

(b) Editions of other relevant texts

ABBO OF ST. GERMAIN, *De Cena Domini*, PL cxxxii. 764.

ÆLFRIC, *Die Hirtenbriefe Ælfrics in altenglischer und lateinischer Fassung*, ed. B. Fehr, Bibliothek der angelsächsischen Prosa, ix (Hamburg, 1914); reprinted, with a Supplement to the Introduction by Peter Clemoes, Darmstadt, 1966.

AMALARIUS OF METZ, *Regula Canonicorum*, ch. 145, PL cv. 932–4.

Anglo-Saxon Laws, F. Liebermann, *Die Gesetze der Angelsächsen* (Halle, 1898–1916).

PSEUDO-ECGBERT, *Penitential: Die altenglische Version des Halitgar'schen Bussbuches*, ed. J. Raith, Bibliothek der ang. Prosa, xiii (1933).

—— *Excerptiones*, ed. B. Thorpe, *Ancient Laws*, pp. 326–42.

LEO IV, *Homilia*, PL cxv. 675–83.

Northumbrian Priests' Law, Gesetze I, 380–3.

PENITENTIALS IN TRANSLATION: J. T. McNeill and H. M. Gamer, *Medieval Handbooks of Penance*, Records of Civilisation, Sources and Studies, xxix (New York, 1938).

PSEUDO-THEODORE, *Penitential*, ed. Thorpe, *Ancient Laws*, pp. 277–306.

THEODULF OF ORLEANS, *Latin Capitula*: PL cv. 191–208.

—— OE. *Capitula* (Bodley 865): ed. A. S. Napier, *The Enlarged Rule of Chrodegang with an Old English version . . . of the Capitula of Theodulf*, E.E.T.S. 1916 (for 1914).

—— OE. *Capitula* (C.C.C.C. 201), ed. B. Thorpe, *Ancient Laws*, pp. 466–88, under the title of 'Ecclesiastical Institutes'.

—— *Additio ad Capitulare*, PL cv. 208–9.

WILLIAM OF MALMESBURY, *Vita Wulfstani*, ed. R. R. Darlington (London, 1928).

WULFSTAN, *The Benedictine Office*:
  ed. E. Feiler, *Das Benediktiner-Offizium*, Anglistische Forschungen, iv (Heidelberg, 1901).
  ed. J. M. Ure, *The Benedictine Office* (Edinburgh, 1957).
—— *Institutes of Polity*:
  ed. Thorpe, *Ancient Laws*, pp. 422–40.
  ed. K. Jost, *Die 'Institutes of Polity'* . . .

WULFSTAN, *Homilies*.
   ed. A. S. Napier, *Wulfstan: Sammlung der ihm zugeschriebenen Homilien nebst Untersuchungen über ihre Echtheit* (Berlin, 1883).
   ed. D. Bethurum, *The Homilies of Wulfstan* (Oxford, 1957).
—— *Sermo Lupi ad Anglos*: ed. D. Whitelock (3rd ed., London, 1963).

II. SECONDARY MATERIAL

(a) Reference Books

ATKINS, I., and KER, N. R., *Catalogus Librorum Manuscriptorum Wigorniensis made in 1622–1623 by Patrick Young* (Cambridge, 1944).
BOSWORTH, J., and TOLLER, T. N., *An Anglo-Saxon Dictionary* (Oxford, 1882–98), *Supplement* (1908–21).
CROSS, F. L., *The Oxford Dictionary of the Christian Church* (Oxford, 1957).
HICKES, G., *Linguarum Veterum Septentrionalium Thesaurus* (1705).
JAMES, M. R., *A Descriptive Catalogue of the Manuscripts in the Library of Corpus Christi College, Cambridge* (Cambridge, 1912).
KER, N. R., *A Catalogue of Manuscripts containing Anglo-Saxon* (Oxford, 1957).
—— *Medieval Libraries of Great Britain* (London, 2nd ed., 1964).
MADAN, F., *A Summary Catalogue of Western Manuscripts in the Bodleian Library* (Oxford, 1922, 1937).
TURNER, C. H., *Early Worcester Manuscripts* (Oxford, 1916).

(b) Works on Wulfstan or relevant to the Canons

ÅNGSTRØM, M., *Studies in Old English Manuscripts* (Uppsala, 1937).
BATESON, M., 'Rules for Monks and Secular Canons after the Revival under King Edgar', *E.H.R.* ix (1894), 690–708.
—— 'The Supposed Latin Penitential of Ecgbert and the Missing Work of Halitgar of Cambrai', *E.H.R.* ix (1894).
—— 'A Worcester Cathedral Book of Ecclesiastical Collections, Made c. 1000 A.D.', *E.H.R.* x (1895), 712–31.
BETHURUM, D., 'Stylistic Features of the Old English Laws', *M.L.R.* xxvii (1932), 263–79.
—— 'Archbishop Wulfstan's Commonplace Book', *P.M.L.A.* lvii (1942), 916–29.
—— 'A Letter of Protest from the English Bishops to the Pope', *Philologica: The Malone Anniversary Studies* (Baltimore, 1949), pp. 97–104.
—— 'Six Anonymous Old English Codes', *J.E.G.Ph.* xlix (1950), 449–63.
CLEMOES, P., 'The Old English Benedictine Office, C.C.C.C. 190, and the relations between Ælfric and Wulfstan: a reconsideration', *Anglia*, lxxviii (1960), 265–83.
—— 'The Chronology of Ælfric's Works', *The Anglo-Saxons. Studies . . . Presented to Bruce Dickins* (London, 1959).
CRAWFORD, S. J., 'The Worcester Marks and Glosses of the Old English Manuscripts in the Bodleian, together with the Worcester version of the Nicene Creed', *Anglia*, lii (1928), 1–25.

BIBLIOGRAPHY

DARLINGTON, R. R., 'Ecclesiastical Reform in the Late Old English Period', *E.H.R.* li (1936), 385–428.

FEHR, B., 'Das Benediktiner-Offizium und die Beziehungen zwischen Ælfric und Wulfstan', *Eng. Stud.* xlvi (1913), 337–47.

FOWLER, R., ' "Archbishop Wulfstan's Commonplace-book" and the *Canons of Edgar*', *Medium Ævum*, xxxii (1963), 1–10.

—— 'A Late Old English Handbook for the use of a Confessor', *Anglia*, lxxxiii (1965), 1–34.

—— 'Some Stylistic Features of the *Sermo Lupi*', *J.E.G.Ph.* lxv (1966), 1–18.

FUNKE, O., 'Some Remarks on Wulfstan's Prose Rhythm', *English Studies*, xliii (1962), 311–18.

GOOLDEN, P., *The Old English Apollonius of Tyre* (Oxford, 1958).

GRENDON, F., *Anglo-Saxon Charms* (New York, 1931).

JOST, K., 'Einige Wulfstantexte und ihre Quellen', *Anglia*, lvi (1932), 265–315.

—— *Wulfstanstudien, Schweizer Anglistische Arbeiten*, xxiii (Bern, 1950).

—— 'Wulfstan und die angelsächsische Chronik', *Anglia*, xlvii (1923), 105–23.

—— Review of Fehr's *Hirtenbriefe, Eng. Stud.* lii (1918), 105 ff.

KER, N. R., 'The Date of the "Tremulous" Worcester Hand', *Leeds Studies in English and Kindred Languages*, vi (1937), 28 ff.

—— 'Hemming's Cartulary', *Studies in Medieval History presented to Frederick Maurice Powicke* (1948), pp. 49–75.

KINARD, J. P., *A Study of Wulfstan's Homilies: Their Style and Sources* (Baltimore, 1897).

KNOWLES, M. D., *The Monastic Order in England* (Oxford, 1949).

LEVIN, S. R., 'On the Authenticity of Five "Wulfstan" Homilies', *J.E.G.Ph.* lx (1961), 451–9.

LIEBERMANN, F., 'Wulfstan und Cnut', *Archiv*, ciii (1899), 47 ff.

MCALISTER, R. A. S., *Ecclesiastical Vestments, their Development and History* (London, 1896).

MCINTOSH, A., 'Wulfstan's Prose', *Proceedings of the British Academy*, xxxv (1949), pp. 109–42.

—— Review of Jost's *Wulfstanstudien, English Studies*, xxxii (1951), 162–8.

MENNER, R. J., 'Anglian and Saxon Elements in Wulfstan's Vocabulary', *M.L.N.* lxiii (1948), 1–9.

OAKLEY, T. P., *English Penitential Discipline and Anglo-Saxon Law in their Joint Influence* (New York, 1923).

POPE, J. C., Review of Bethurum's *The Homilies of Wulfstan*, *M.L.N.* lxxiv (1959).

ROUNDELL, Earl of Selborne, *Ancient Facts and Fictions concerning Churches and Tithes* (1892).

SCHLEMILCH, W., *Beiträge zur Sprache und Orthographie spätaltengl. Sprachdenkmäler der Übergangszeit, 1000–1150* (*Studien zur englischen Philologie*, xxxiv, 1914).

SELDEN, J., *The History of Tithes*. (Vol. 3 of *Joannis Seldeni . . . opera omnia . . . collegit David Wilkins*, 1726.)
SISAM, K., *Studies in the History of Old English Literature* (Oxford, 1953).
STENTON, F. M., *Anglo-Saxon England* (2nd ed., Oxford, 1947).
STUBBS, W., *Memorials of St. Dunstan* (*Rolls Series*, 63, 1874).
WATKINS, O. D., *A History of Penance* (London, 1920).
WHITBREAD, L., 'MS. C.C.C.C. 201: A Note on its Character and Provenance', *Philological Quarterly*, xxxviii (1959), 106–12.
WHITELOCK, D., 'A Note on the Career of Wulfstan the Homilist', *E.H.R.* lii (1937), 460–5.
—— 'Wulfstan and the so called Laws of Edward and Guthrum', *E.H.R.* lvi (1941), 1–21.
—— 'Archbishop Wulfstan, Homilist and Statesman', *T.R.H.S.* 4th series, xxiv (1942), 25–45.
—— 'Two Notes on Ælfric and Wulfstan', *M.L.R.* xxxviii (1943).
—— 'Wulfstan and the Laws of Cnut', *E.H.R.* lxiii (1948), 433–52.
—— 'Wulfstan's Authorship of Cnut's Laws', *E.H.R.* lxx (1955), 72–85.
—— (ed.) *English Historical Documents*, i (London, 1955).
—— 'Wulfstan at York', in *Franciplegius: Medieval and Linguistic Studies in Honor of Francis Peabody Magoun, Jr.*, ed. Jess B. Bessinger, Jr., and Robert P. Creed (New York, 1965), pp. 214–31.

GLOSSARY

The forms of words are as in D, except where reconstructed head-words have to be given; in these cases the full spelling of the form in the text follows, with morphological identification. Additional words in X are noted, with an X before the section number; but minor orthographic variants from D in X, and consistent variants, such as D -i- for X -y-, are not noted. Numerical references are to sections of the text; where a word occurs frequently, 'etc.' is added after one or two examples. ge- is ignored in the alphabetical listing; æ comes after *a*, not between *ad* and *af*; ð and þ are conflated after *t*. Abbreviations are conventional.

ā *adv.* always 1, 38, 42; aa 52, X67.
ābirigan *w.2* partake of: ābirige *pres. subj. 3s.* 36.
ac *conj.* but 4, 7, 8, etc.
ācweðan 5 respond: ācweðe *pret. subj. 3s.* 35.
ādwǣscan *w.1* put down: ādwǣsce *pres. subj. 3s.* 16.
āgan *irreg.*: nāh *neg. pres. 3s.* ought not 22.
āgen *adj.* own: -ne *mnp.* 7.
alba *m.* alb: -n *ds.* 33.
ān (1) *num.* one: -es *mgs.* 37; -e *fas.* 48; -ra *fds.* 13: ǣnne *mas.* X56; (2) *adj.* alone: -a *mns.* 35; (3) *adv.* alike, as one 50; (4) *adv.* once: ǣne X41.
and *conj.* and 1, 2, 3, etc.
andettan *w.1* confess: andette *pres. subj. 3s.* 68.
ānfeald *adj.* single: -re *fds.* X68e, f.
ānrǣd *adj.* of one mind: -e *mnp.* 1, 48.
ārǣran *w.1* raise, foster: ārǣre *pres. subj. 3s.* 16.
ariht *adv.* correctly 13.
ārwurðlice *adv.* reverently 42.
ārwurðnes *f.* reverence: -se *ds.* 26.
āsmēan *w.1* consider: āsmēað *pres. 3s.* 13.
āð *m.* oath: -as *ap.* 24, 60.
āðfultum *m.* support for an oath: *as.* X68h.
axse *fp.* ashes: axsan *ap.* 38, axan X43.
ǣfen *m.* eve: *as.* X54.

ǣfre *adv.* ever 26, 31, 32, etc.
ǣfter *prep. w. dat.* after 68.
ǣghwār *adv.* everywhere 15.
ǣghwilc *pron.* every: -e *fas.* 69.
ǣgðer ge . . . ge *conj.* both . . . and 55, 69.
ǣlc *pron.* each 1, 2, 5, etc.
ǣlmesse *f.* alms: ǣlmessan *as. or p.* 55, 57; *dp.* 49.
ǣlmihtig *adj.* almighty 69; -es *mgs.* 4.
ǣne see ān (4).
ǣni(g) *pron.* any 5, 6, 8, etc.
ǣr (1) *adv.* previously 10; ǣrest *supl.* first 54; (2) *conj.* before 22.
ǣt *prep. w. dat.* at, from 16, 22, 28, etc.
ǣtdōn *irreg.* deprive (of): ǣtdō *pres. subj. 3s.* 9.
ǣtforan *prep. w. dat.* before 32.
geǣðe *pres. subj. 3s.* of *(ge)āðan? confirm by an oath 63; *see* Commentary.

be *prep. w. dat.* (1) concerning *heading* D; (2) at 54; (3) according to X68b.
be þām þe *conj.* if 22, 47.
beard *m.* beard: *as.* 47.
bearn *n.* child: *as.* 17.
bebirgan *w.2* bury: bebirge *pres. subj. 3s.* 68.
bēc(c) see bōc.
gebed *n.* prayer: -um *dp.* 70.
befeallan 7 fall: befealenne *pret. p. mas.* 6.
behweorfan 3 put in order, arrange: behweorfe *pres. subj. 3s.* 68;

behworfen *pret. p.* 33; behworfene *pret. p. nnp.* 42.
belēan 6 dissuade from *or* deprecate:
  pres. subj. 3p. 58.
belecgan *w.1* charge, accuse: belecġe
  pres. subj. 3s. X68e, g, h, i; belēde
  pret. subj. 3s. X68c.
bēodan 2 (1) offer: ġebudon *pret.
  3p.* 39; (2) command: bēode *pres.
  subj. 3s.* 15; bēodan *pres. subj. 3p.*
  48.
bēon, wesan *irreg.* be 22; bið *pres.
  3s.* 69, is 39, 61; bēo *pres. subj. 3s.*
  5, 7, 14, sī, sȳ 1, 7, 15, etc.; bēon
  pres. subj. 3p. 1, 48, sȳn 13; wæs
  pret. 3s. 8; wǣre *pret. subj. 3s.*
  X68i; nǣre *neg. pret. subj. 3s.* X68c.
beorgan 3: beorgan wið *pres. subj.
  3p.* keep (themselves) from 58, 60.
beran 4: mid beran take on X68i.
besēon 5 look: besēo *pres. subj. 3s.*
  32.
bet *adv. comp.* better 12.
(ġe)bētan *w.1* (1) amend, improve:
  ġebēte *pres. subj. 3s.* 5, 12; (2) make
  amends X68i; bēte *pres. subj. 3s.* 38.
betǣcan *w.1* allot: betǣce *pres. subj.
  3s.* X56.
betweox *prep. w. dat.* between 7, 23.
(ġe)biddan 5 (1) exhort: biddan
  pres. subj. 3p. 57; (2) pray: ġebidde
  pres. subj. 3s. 28; ġebiddan *pres.
  subj. 3p.* 45.
ġebīgan *w.1* compel 6.
binnan, binnon *prep. w. dat.* within
  15, 26, 46.
ġebird *f.* birth: -a *ds.* 13.
biriġan *w.2* bury: biriġe *pres. subj.
  3s.* 29.
ġebir(i)ġan *w.2* belong to, be appropriate to: ġebirað *pres. 3s.* heading
  D, 59, 65; ġebiriġe *pres. subj. 3s.* 9,
  39; ġebirgan *pres. subj. 3p.* 42.
bisǣce *adj.* disputed 63; see *Commentary.*
biscop *m.* bishop 5; *as.* 70; -e *ds.* 7;
  -es *gs.* 22; bisceop *ns.* X65, X66.
bismer *n.* insult: *as.* 39.
bismorlic *adj.* shameful: -ra *fgp.* 20.
bisni(ġ)an *w.2* set an example:
  bisniġe *pres. subj. 3s.* 69; bisnian
  pres. subj. 3p. 52.
bīwist *f.* provisions, food: -e *as.* 3.

blæc *n.* ink: *as.* 3.
bletsian *w.2* consecrate: ġebletsod
  pret. p. 8.
bletsung *f.* blessing: -e *as.* 47.
blōd *n.* blood: *as.* 53.
bōc *f.* book: bēc *ds.* 32; bēcc *ap.* 3,
  34; bōcum *dp.* 65.
bōcfel *n.* parchment: *as.* 3.
bodiġan *w.2* preach: bodiġe *pres.
  subj. 3s.* 69; bodiġan *pres. subj. 3p.*
  52.
bōt *f.* atonement, penance: -e *ds.* 6,
  68.
ġebringan *w.1* put: ġebringe *pres.
  subj. 3s.* 38, X43.
brūcan 2 *w. gen.* use 38.
būte *conj.* unless 29.
būton, būtan (1) *prep. w. dat.* without
  10, 32, 46, etc.; (2) *conj.* unless,
  except 30, 31, 36, etc.
byrnende *adj.* (*pres. p. of* byrnan)
  burning: *nns.* 42.

calic *m.* chalice 41.
candelmæsse *f.* Candlemas: *as.*?
  X54.
cann see cunnan.
canon *m.* canon 32; canon law X65.
cifesġemāna *m.* adultery: -n *gs.* 21.
cild *n.* child 15, *ap.* X16.
cirice *f.* church 61: circan *as.* 8, *ds.*
  27, *gs.* 46; cirican *as. or p.* 26.
circfultum *m.* help at church: *as.* 51.
ciricsceat *m. see Commentary* 54.
cirictūn *m.* churchyard: -e *ds.* 26.
ciricþēnung *f.* church duty, service:
  -um *dp.* 50.
ciricwæcce *f.* vigil: ciricwæccan
  ds. 28.
clǣne *adj.* pure: *nns.* 39, *fns.* 39;
  clǣnan *mds.* 26; clǣnum *nds.* 38.
clǣnlīce *adv.* purely 42.
clǣnnes *f.* purity: -se *ds.* 38.
cleric *m.* clerk: *as.* 4; clerec *ns.* X65.
cniht *m.* servant: -e *ds.* 4.
corporalem *see Commentary* 33.
corsnǣd *f.* 'trial piece': -e *ds.* X68h,
  i; *see Commentary.*
cræft *m.* skill, *as.* X16: -an *dp.* 51.
crēda *m.* the Creed: crēdon *as.* 17,
  22.
crisma *m.* chrism: -n *as.* 70.
cristen *adj.* Christian 17, 22, etc.

GLOSSARY

cristendōm m. Christianity: as. 16, 69; -e ds. 17.
cuman 4 come: cume pres. subj. 3s. 26, 42, 44, 46.
cunnan irreg. know: cann pres. 3s. 22; cunne pres. subj. 3s. 12, 22.
ġecwĕman w.1 please: ġecwĕme pres. subj. 3s. 29 (ġecwĕmde pret. X29).
ġecwĕme adj. pleasing, nns. X49: ġecwĕmre comp. nns. 49.
cyngc m. king: as. 70.
cȳpinġ f. marketing: -e gs. 19.
cyricnēod f. needs of the church: -e ds. X56.
(ġe)cȳðan w.1 say: cȳðanne infl. inf. 70; ġecȳðe pres. subj. 3s. 5, 6.

dǣd f. deed X68b: -e as. 26.
dǣdbana m. evil-doer X68i.
dǣdbōt f. penance: -e as. 68.
dæġ m. day: -es gs. 37; daga gp. 3.
dǣl m. part: as. X56.
dǣlan w.1 share out: pres. subj. 3p. 55, 57.
dearr irreg. dare: durre pres. subj. 3s. 6, X68e.
dēman w.1 decree: ġedēmde pret. 3s. X68c.
dēofol m. devil: dēofles gs. 18, X16.
deriġan w.1 w. dat. injure: deriġe pres. subj. 3s. 5.
diacon m. deacon X65, X68g.
didon see dōn.
disiġ n. foolishness: as. 4.
dislic adj. foolish: -ra npg. 20.
dōn irreg. do 54; dēð pres. 3s. 39; dō pres. subj. 3s. 69; dōn pres. subj. 3p 55; didon pret. 3p. 39; ġedōn pret. p. 5, 70.
ġedrenc see ġedrync.
drēogan 2 (1) perform: drȳhð, drīhð, pres. 3s. X16; drēogað pres. 3p. 16; drēogan pres. subj. 3p. 50; (2) allow: drēoġe pres. subj. 3s. 28.
ġedrēoh adj. sober 28.
drīfan 1 carry out: drīfð pres. 3s. 16.
drīhð see drēogan.
ġedryh X26: for ġedrync as. D26, or ġedryþ f. 'action, behaviour'?
drȳhð see drēogan.
ġedrync m. drinking: as. 26; ġedrenc as. 28.

durre see dearr.
duru f. door: dyre ds. 46.
dwelian w.2 mislead: pres. subj. 3p. 48.
ġedwimer n. delusion: -um dp. 16.
dyre see duru.

ēac conj. also 16, 60, 68, 69.
ēaġe n. eye: ēaġum dp. 32.
eal adj. all 1, 4, 5, etc.; mid ealle adv entirely 16.
ealascop m. ale-poet 59.
eald adj. old: yldrum comp. mdp. as noun elders 2.
ealdor m. master: ealdre ds. 1.
ealles adv. all, altogether 23, 61.
eallswā conj. just the same as X68c.
ēastron dp. Easter 54.
eced m. vinegar: as. 39.
efenboren adj. born equal X68c.
efenforð adj. equally advanced: -e mnp. X50.
efenweorð adj. equally honoured: -e mnp. 50.
efesung f. hair-style: -a gp. 20.
eft adv. again 40.
eġe m. fear: ds. 4, 45, 68.
ellen n. elder-tree: -um dp. 16.
elles adv. otherwise X43.
eorðe f. earth, soil: eorðan as. X16.
eorðwestm f. fruit of the earth: -a np. 54.
ēst f. grace, will: on Godes ēst according to God's will 49.

fadiġan w.2 organize, live (one's life): fadiġe pres. subj. 3s. X68b.
faran 6 proceed: pres. subj. 3p. 4; fare pres. subj. 3s. X65.
fæc n. time: -e ds. 50.
ġefæd n.? decorum: -e ds. 4.
ġefæd adj. orderly: -ne mas. 4.
fǣhð f. enmity: -a as. X68i.
fæsten n. fast 49; -an dp. 48.
fæsten n. sanctuary: as. X68i.
fæstendæġ m. fast-day: fæstendaġum dp. 24.
feccan w.1 fetch: fecce pres. subj. 3s. 70.
fela w. gen. many 16.
ġefēra m. companion: -n np. 7.
filstan w.1 help: filste pres. subj. 3s. 68; ġefilstan tō pres. subj. 3p. 5.
fȳr n. fire: -e ds. 38, fȳre X43.

GLOSSARY

firðrigan *w.2* further: firðrige *pres. subj. 3s.* 69.
flǣsc *n.* meat: *as.* X65.
geflit *n.* strife 23.
folc *n.* people: *as.* 1, 45, 48, etc.; -es *gs.* X54.
folcgemōt *n.* assembly: -a *gp.* 19.
folcisc *adj.* secular: -ne *mas.* X68g.
folgian *w.2* be subject to, obey: folgode *pret. 3s.* 10.
fōn . . . on 7 take on, take up, go to: *pres. subj. 3p.* 5: on . . . fō *pres. subj. 3s.* X68i.
for *prep. w. acc.* for, on behalf of, 1, 45, 70; *w. dat.* before 1, because of 6, 30, 36.
forāð *m.* oath before (dispute), guarantee: -e *ds.* 64.
forbærnan *w.1* destroy by burning: forbærne *pres. subj. 3s.* 38, X43.
forbēodan 2 forbid: forbēode *pres. subj. 3s.* 16, forbēodan *pres. subj. 3p.* 60.
fore *adv.* on someone's account X68i.
for(h)ealdi(g)an *w.2* (decay with) age: forealdige *pres. subj. 3s.* 38; forhealden *pret. p.* 38 *see Commentary.*
forgān *irreg.* forgo, do without: forgā *pres. subj. 3s.* 24, 25.
forgīman *w.1* neglect: forgīme *pres. subj. 3s.* 43; forgīmde *pret. 3s.* 38.
forhealden *see* for(h)ealdi(g)an.
forlǣtan 7 desert: forlǣte *pres. subj. 3s.* 8.
forsēon 5 despise: forsēo *pres. subj. 3s.* 13.
forðām *conj.* because: X13, 22, X39.
forðboren *adj.* of noble birth 13.
forðsīð *m.* death: -e *ds.* 68.
frēols *m.* feast-day: -an *dp.* 48.
frēolsdæg *m.* festival: frēolsdagum *dp.* 18, 23, 24.
frēolstīd *f.* festival: -um *dp.* 15.
frēondlēas *adj.* friendless: -ne *mas.* X68h.
friðsplott *m.* 'peace-place': -um *dp.* 16 *see Commentory.*
fūl *adj.* impure: *nas.* 39; -es *ngs. as noun* X42.
full *adj.* full: -es *mgs.* X68b, d.
fullian *w.2* baptize: gefullod *pret. p.* 15.

fulluht *n.* baptism: -es *gs.* 15; -e *ds.* 22.
fulluhtele *m.* baptismal oil: *as.* 69.
fultum *m.* assistance: -e *ds.* 1.

gaderian *w.2* assemble: gegaderod *pret. p.* X54.
galdor *n.* spell: galdra *ap.* 16.
gamen *n.* game: -a *gp.* 18.
gān *irreg.* go: gā *pres. subj. 3s.* X68h, i.
gangdagas *mp.* Rogation days: gangdagum *dp.* X54.
ge . . . ge *conj.* both . . . and 1.
gealla *m.* gall: -n *as.* 39.
gēar *n.* year: -es *gs.* 50; -e *ds.* 3.
geara *adj.* ready 69; *nns.* 38; gearuwe *mnp.* X67.
geoguð *f.* youth: -e *as.* 51; geoguð tēoðung 54 *see Commentary.*
geong *adj.* young: gingran *comp. mnp. as noun* novices 2.
georne *adv.* eagerly, willingly 2, 11 34, *etc.*
geornlīce *adv.* eagerly, zealously 1, 16, 17.
gif *conj.* if 5, 6, 7, *etc.*
gildscipe *m.* gild: *ds.* 9 *see Commentary.*
gingran *see* geong.
girnan *w.1 w. gen.* beg, desire: girne *pres. subj. 3s.* 15; girnan *pres. subj. 3p.* 68.
gitsigende *adj.* avaricious, covetous 14.
gegladian *w.2* please 55.
glīwigan *w.2* make merry: glīwige *pres. subj. 3s.* 59.
God *m.* God 1, 4, 6, *etc.*
gōd *adj.* good: -e *fap.* 34.
godcund *adj.* divine: -re *fds.* 3, 26.
gegoten *adj.* (*pret. p.*) made of metal 41.

habban *irreg.* have 47: habbe *pres. subj. 3s.* 33, hæbbe 4, 8, 34, etc.; habban *pres. subj. 3p.* 3, 51; hæfde *pret. 3s.* X68c; næbbe *neg. pres. subj. 3s.* 35.
hād *m.* order (of a priest): -e *ds.* 59, 65.
gehāda *m.* one of the same rank: -n *ap.* 68f, *dp.* 68e.
gehādod *adj.* (*pret. p.*) in holy orders

GLOSSARY

47, X65, X66; -ra *mgp. heading* D.
hafecere *m.* hawker 65.
hālga *m.* saint: **hālgena** *gp.* X54.
hālgigan *w.2* consecrate: **hālgige** *pres. subj. 3s.* 40, 41.
gehālgod *adj.* (*from above*) consecrated: *nas.* 40, 43; **-re** *fds.* 30; **-an** *nds.* 22; **-on** *nds.* 31.
hālig *adj.* holy: *nas.* 43; **-es** *ngs. as noun* 43.
hāligdōm *m.* sacrament: *as.* 42.
hand *f.* hand: **-a** *ds.* 22.
handcræft *m.* manual skill: *as.* 11.
hæbbe *see* **habban.**
hǣþen *adj.* heathen, pagan: **-ra** *ngp.* 18.
hǣþendōm *m.* paganism: *as.* 16.
hē *pron.* he 6, 8, 29; **hine** *as.* 12, 47; **his** *gs.* 4, 6, 9, *etc.*; **hys** *gs.* 9; **him** *ds.* 5, 8, 32, *etc.*, **heom** 5, **hym** 35; **hit** *nns.* 5, 13, 38, *etc.*; **his** *gs.* 15, 38; **hī(g)** *np.* 1, 3, 5, *etc.*; **hī** *ap.* 68; **heora** *gp.* 1, 2, 7, *etc.*; **him** *dp.* 17, 60, **heom** 5, 68.
hēafodleahter *m.* mortal sin: **hēafodleahtrum** *dp.* 6.
healdan 7 keep, look after: **healde** *pres. subj. 3s.* 38, **healdan** *3p.* 26.
hēalīce *adv.* greatly 5.
heligan *w.2* conceal: **helige** *pres. subj. 3s.* 47.
help *f.* help: **-e** *ds.* 1.
heom, heora *see* **hē.**
hēr *adv.* here *heading* D.
hī(g) *see* **hē.**
higelēas *adj.* foolish: **-ra** *ngp.* 20.
him, his, hit *see* **hē.**
hlāf *m.* bread: *as.* 43.
hold *adj.* loyal: **-e** *mnp.* 1.
hors *n.* horse X26.
hrihtlīce *see* **rihtlīce.**
hringan *see* **ringan.**
hund *n.* dog 26.
hunta *m.* huntsman 65.
huntaþ *m.* hunting: *as.* X65.
hūru *adv.* certainly, indeed 31, 34, 46.
hūs *n.* house: **-e** *ds.* 30.
hūsl *n.* eucharist: *as.* 38, 40, 41; **-es** *gs.* 22, 36; **-e** *ds.* 39.
hūsligan *w.2* give eucharist to: **hūslige** *pres. subj. 3s.* 68.
gehwā *pron.* everyone 49.
hwat *n.* augury: **-a** *ap.* 16.

hwæt *pron.* (1) anything: *nns.* 5; (2) what: *nas.* 70.
hwīl *f.* time: **-e** *ds.* 47; **þā hwīle þe** *conj.* whilst 44.
(ge)hwilc *pron.* each, every 4, 11, 14, *etc*; **hwilces** *mgs.* any 30.
hȳran *w.1* obey: *pres. subj. 3p.* 2.
gehȳrsum *adj.* obedient: **-e** *mnp.* 1.
hys *see* **hē.**

īdel *adj.* idle: **-e** *fas.* 26; *as noun* 26.
innan *prep. w. dat.* within 26, 29.
inne *adv.* inside 26.
intō *prep. w. dat.* into 27.
is *see* **bēon.**

lād *f.* defence (in law): **-e** *as.*? X68c.
lādi(g)an *w.2* defend (in law), clear (oneself) X68h; **lādige** *pres. subj. 3s.* 64, X68e, g, *etc.*
lagu *f.* law: **lage** *as.* X68b.
lange *adv.* long 15.
lār *f.* learning *or* teaching: **-e** *ds.* 11.
lǣran *w.1* (1) decree: **lǣrað** *pres. 1p.* 1, 2, *etc.*; (2) teach; **lǣran** *pres. subj. 3p.* 2, 51.
gelǣred *adj.* learned 12.
lǣs *adv. comp.* (less): **þī lǣs þe** *conj.* in case 32.
lǣsboren *adj.* of less noble birth: **-an** *mas.* 13.
lǣtan 7 (1) judge: **lǣte** *pres. subj. 3s.* 29; (2) allow: **lǣte** *pres. subj. 3s.* 47.
lǣwed *adj. as noun* layman X68c.
lēaf *f.* permission: **-e** *ds.* 10.
gelēanian *w.2* reward: **gelēanað** *pres. 3s.* 69.
lēas *adj.* false: **-re** *fds.* 62.
leger *n.* grave: **-es** *gs.* 29.
lēofost *adj. supl.* most pleasing 69.
lēoht *n.* light 42.
lēohtgesceot *n.* light-dues: **-u** *ap.* X54 *see Commentary.*
(ge)leorni(g)an *w.2* learn 22: **leornige** *pres. subj. 3s.* 11, 22.
lēoð *n.* song: **-a** *gp.* 18.
libban *w.1* live: **libbe** *pres. subj. 3s.* X68e, f, g.
līc *n.* body: **-e** *ds.* 68.
gelīce *prep. w. dat.* like 39.
licgan 5 lie 22.
līcwiglung *f.* necromancy: **-a** *ap.* 16.
līf *n.* life: **-e** *ds.* 29.

GLOSSARY

līffadung *f.* way of life: **-e** *ds.* heading D.
(ge)lōgian *w.2* put: **lōgige** *pres. subj. 3s.* 27, **gelōge** 42.
lufi(g)an *w.2* love: **lufige** *pres. subj. 3s.* 4, 21, *etc.*; **lufian** *pres. subj. 3p.* 2.

mā *adv. comp.* more 26; **mǣst** *supl.* 37.
magan *irreg.* be able: **mǣge** *pres. subj. 3s.* 6, 26, 38.
man *m.* man *heading* D, 4, 5, *etc.*; **men** *np.* 16, *ap.* 68.
man *indef. pron.* one 7, 13, 15, *etc.*
maneg *adj.* many: **-um** *ndp.* 16.
mangere *m.* merchant 14.
manweorðung *f.* worship of humans: **-a** *ap.* 16.
massere *m.* trader 14.
mǣg *m.* kinsman: **māgum** *dp.* X68i.
mǣge *see* **magan**.
mǣglēas *adj.* without kin X68i.
gemǣne *adj.* common: **gemǣnre** *fds.* 1.
mǣngan *w.1* mix: **mǣngdon** *pret. 3p.* 39.
mǣsse *f.* mass: **mǣssan** *as.* 42, *ds.* 54.
mǣssepreost *m.* priest 35, X65, X66; **-a** *gp.* 46.
mǣsserēaf *n.* vestments: *as.* 33.
mǣssi(g)an *w.2* say mass 39: **mǣssige** *pres. subj. 3s.* 30, 31, 32, *etc.*
mǣst *see* **mā**, **micel**.
gemearr *n.* error: *ap.* 16.
micel *adj.*; *sup. as noun* **mǣst**, X54.
mid *prep. w. dat.* with 4, 14, 45, *etc.*
midd *adj.* mid: **-an** *mds.* X54.
misbēodan *2* injure, ill-use: **misboden** *pret. p.* 5.
misefesian *w.2* cut (someone's) hair wrongly 47.
misfadigan *w.2* live sinfully: **misfadige** *pres. subj. 3s.* X68b.
missan *w.1* (miss): **þī lǣs þe him misse** *pres. subj. 3s.* in case he forgets 32.
mistlic *adj.* various: **-um** *ndp.* 16.
mōnað *m.* month X65.
mōt *irreg.* be allowed: **mōtan** *pres. subj. 3p.* X68i.
mynegian *w.2* remind: *pres. subj. 3p.* 54.

mynster *n.* church: **mynstre** *ds.* 9.
mynsterprēost *m.* parish priest?: **-a** *gp.* 46 *see Commentary*.

nā *adv.* never, not at all 16, 38.
nāh see **āgan**.
nān *adj.* no 9, 26, *etc.*; **nǣnne** *mas.* X41.
nāðor ne ... ne *conj.* neither ... nor X68b.
nǣbbe see **habban**.
nǣfre *adv.* never 39, 40.
nǣnig *pron.* no, none: **-ne** *mas.* 4.
nǣre see **bēon**.
ne (1) *adv.* not 6, 7, 8, *etc.*; (2) *conj.* nor 14, 26, 65, *etc.*
nēah *prep. w. dat.* near 42, 44.
nēawyst, -west *f.* neighbourhood: **-wyste** *as.* 61, **-weste** *ds.* 16.
nele see **willan**.
niht *f.* night; *as.* X16; *p.* (measurement of time) days 54; **-um** *dp.* 15.
niman *5* take: **nime** *pres. subj. 3s.* X68f.
notian *w.2 w. gen.* use X43.
nū *adv.* now *heading* D.
nȳde *adv.* of necessity 7.

ofer *prep. w. dat. or acc.* through X50, after X54.
oferdrincan *3* drink too much: **oferdrince** *pres. subj. 3s.* X66.
oferdruncen *n.* drunkenness: *as.* 58.
oferhȳre *adj.* disobedient 6.
ofersēocnes *f.* serious illness: **-se** *ds.* 30, 36.
oferslipe *m.* 46 *see Commentary*.
oferslop *n.* X46 *see Commentary*.
oflete *f.* sacramental wafer 39.
oft X43 *see Commentary*.
oftor *adv. comp.* more often 37, X41.
on *prep. w. dat. or acc.* on, in 6, 26, 39, *etc.*
onfōn *7* receive: **onfōnne** *infl. inf.* 22.
onginnan *3* begin: **onginð** *pres. 3s.* 39.
onufan *prep. w. dat.* upon 31, after 54.
ordel, ordol *n.* ordeal: **ordela** *ap.* 24, **ordol** *as.* 63.
ōðer (1) *pron.* other 1, 2, 9; (2) *adj.* second; **-ne** *mas.* X54; **ōðre sīðe** *adv.* second, next X54.

GLOSSARY

oððe *conj.* or 6, 7, 22; opðon X22; oððe ... oððe either ... or X66.

plegian *w.2* play, amuse: **plegge** *pres. subj. 3s.* 65.
prēost *m.* priest 4, 5, 6, *etc.*

rǣd *m.* conduct: -a *gp.* 20.
rǣdan *w.1* decide: **rǣde** *pres. subj. 3s.* X68i.
gerǣde *n.* ornaments: **gerǣda** *gp.* 20.
rǣdlīce *adv.* deliberately X66.
gerǣdnes *f.* instruction *heading* D; -sum *dp.* 3.
rēaf *n.* garments, vestments: *as.* 3.
regollīce *adv.* regularly, according to a (monastic) way of life X68e, f.
regollīf *n.* regular life: *as.* X68g.
riht *n.* (right): *ds.* **mid rihte** according to right 22.
riht *adj.* rightful, correct: -ne *mas.* 45; -e *fap.* 34.
rihtǣwe *n.* lawful wife: *as.* 8, 21, 61.
gerihte *n.* due: **gerihtum** *dp.* 69, **gerihtan** 54; **gerihtum** *dp.* X67 needs.
rihtfæstendæg *m.* proper fast: **rihtfæstendagum** *dp.* 23.
rihtfæstentīd *f.* proper fast: -um *dp.* 25.
rihtlīce *adv.* rightly 14; **hrihtlīce** X68d.
ringan *3* ring: **ringe** *pres. subj. 3s.* 45, **hrincge** X45.
Rōmfeoh *n.* Peter's Pence 54.

sacerd *m.* priest: *as.* X68e.
sacu *f.* strife 7.
samlǣred *adj.* half-educated: -an *mas.* 12.
scaru *f.* tonsure: **scare** *as.* 47.
scændan *w.1* scorn: **scænde** *pres. subj. 3s.* 12.
scēotan *2* pass: *pres. subj. 3p.* 7; **gescoten** *pret. p.* 7.
scolere *m.* novice: *as.* 10.
scrīfan *1* hear confession: **scrīfe** *pres. subj. 3s.* 68.
scrift *m.* penance: -es *gs.* X15.
scriftscīr *f.* parish: -e *ds.* 6, 9, 15.
sculan *irreg.* be obliged to: **scoldan** *pres. 3p.* 16; **scule** *pres. subj. 3s.* 7; **sculan** *pres. subj. 3p.* 54.

se *def. art. and pron.* 22, 38, *etc.*; **þone** *mas.* 12, 13, 42, **þæne** X68c; **þæs** *mgs.* 10; **ðām** *mds.* 7, 38; **sēo** *fns.* X68b; **þā** *fas.* 8, 44, 57; **þāre** *fds.* 46; **þæt** *nas.* 7, 22, 40; **þæs** *ngs.* 29, **þæs þe** *as.* 26 which 27; **þām** *nds.* 46; **þī, þe** *nis. before comp.* the, any 26, 32; **þā** *np.* 2, 42, *ap.* 38; **þāra** *gp.* 9, 37.
sealm *m.* psalm: -as *ap.* 57.
sealt *n.* salt: *as.* 43.
gesēcan *w.1* go to: **gesēce** *pres. subj. 3s.* 45.
secgan *w.1* say: **segð** *pres. 3s.* X65; **secge** *pres. subj. 3s.* X68i.
sēman *w.1* reconcile: *pres. subj. 3p.* 7.
sēoc *adj.* sick: -e *map.* 68; -um *mdp. as noun* 69.
sēofeða *num.* seventh X68f.
sī see **bēon**.
sibbian *w.2* make peace: *pres. subj. 3p.* 7.
silf *adj.* himself 40; -um *mds.* 59.
silfwilles *adv.* deliberately 8.
sillan *w.1* give: **sille** *pres. subj. 3s.* 49.
singan *3* sing, celebrate (mass): **singe** *pres. subj. 3s.* 42; **singan** *pres. subj. 3p.* 57.
sinoð *m.* synod: -e *ds.* 3, 4, 5; **synoðe** *ds.* 6.
sīðe X54 see **ōðer** (2).
siððan *adv.* afterwards 39.
six *num.* six X68f.
smerigan *w.2* anoint: **smerige** *pres. subj. 3s.* 68.
smyrels *m.* ointment: *as.* 69.
sōm *f.* arbitration: -e *ds.* 7.
sōna swā *conj.* as soon as 15.
sp(r)ǣc *f.* speech: **spǣce** *as.* 26; **sprǣce** *ds.* X68e, f.
stān *m.* stone: -um *dp.* 16.
standan *6* stand: **stande** *pres. subj. 3s.* 62.
stānwurðung *f.* worship of stones: -a *as.* X16.
stor *m.* frankincense: *as.* 43.
subumlem 33 see *Commentary*.
subumbrale X33 see *Commentary*.
sulhælmesse *f.* plough-alms: **sulhælmessan** *np.* 54 see *Commentary*.
sumer *m.* summer: -a *ds.* X54.

GLOSSARY

sunnandæg *m.* Sunday: -es *gs.* 19; -e *ds.* 52.
swā (1) *conj.* as 5, 59, 65; (2) *adv.* so 55.
geswīcan *1 w. gen.* avoid, eschew: geswīce *pres. subj. 3s.* 18, 19, 20, *etc.*
swilce, *conj.* as if 5.
swīðe *adv.* much, greatly, very 23, 28, 42, *etc.*
swȳn *n.* pig 26.
sȳ, sȳn *see* bēon.
synoðe *see* sinoð.

(ge)tǣcan *w.1* (1) teach: tǣce *pres. subj. 3s.* 17; (2) command: getǣce *pres. subj. 3s.* 5; (3) impose: tǣce *pres. subj. 3s.* 68.
tǣcincg *f.* teaching: -e *ds.* X68b.
tæflere *m.* gambler 65.
tēon *2* (1) drag: tīhð *pres. 3s.* X16; (2) instruct: tēon *pres. subj. 3p.* 51.
tēoðung *f.* tithe: -e *np.* 54; -um *dp.* 54.
tīd *f.* (canonical) hour: -a *ap.* 45.
tīdsang *m.* service: *as.* 45.
tihtle *f.* accusation: tihtlan *ds.* X68c, e, g.
tihtligan *w.2* accuse: tihtlige *pres. subj. 3s.* X68f.
tiligan *w.2* provide for: tilige *pres. subj. 3s.* 14, 34.
tīma *m.* time: -n *as.* 45.
tīðigan *w.2 w. gen.* grant: tīðige *pres. subj. 3s.* 15.
tō (1) *prep. w. dat.* in, to, for 1, 3, 54, *etc.*; (2) too 15, 23, 61.
tō ðām *adv.* so 29.
tōēacan *prep. w. dat.* besides 1.
tōgædere *adv.* together 39.
trēow *n.* tree: -um *dp.* 16.
trēowen *adj.* wooden: -um *mds.* 41.
trēowwurðung *f.* worship of trees: -a *ap.* X16.
getrȳwe *adj.* loyal: *mnp.* 1.
twēgen *num.* two: *map.* X68f; twā *nap.* X65; twām *dp.* X68e.

þā *see* se.
þā *conj.* when 39.
geþafi(g)an *w.2* allow: geþafige *pres. subj. 3s.* 68; geþafian *pres. subj. 3p.* X68e.

ðām *see* se.
þār *adv.* there 26, 28, 39, *etc.*
þāra, þāre *see* se.
þārtō *adv.* thereto 27.
þæne *see* se.
þǣræt *adv.* thereat X68i.
þæs, þæt *see* se.
þæt *conj.* (1) that 1, 2, 3, *etc.*; (2) so that 5.
þe *see* se.
þe *rel. part.* who, which 4, 6, 7.
þearf *f.* need 38, 68; -e *ds.* 1.
þearfa *m.* poor (man): -n *ap.* 57; -um *dp.* X56.
þegnscipe *m.* status of a thane: -s *gs.* X68b.
þegn *m.* 'thane'; *here* secular freeman as opposed to cleric: *as.* 64; -es *gs.* 64.
þēnigan *w.2* serve: þēnige *pres. subj. 3s.* 46; þēnigende *pres. p.* 1.
þēnung *f.* service: -e *ds.* 3, 26.
þēof *m.* thief: -a *gp.* 62.
þēow *m.* servant, minister: -as *np.* 1.
þēowdōm *m.* service: -e *ds.* 26.
þēowigan *w.2* serve: þēowigende *pres. p.* 1.
(ge)þicgan *5* partake of, taste: (ge)þicge *pres. subj. 3s.* 40, 53.
þing(c) *n.* thing 9, 26, 39, *etc.*
þingi(g)an *w.2* intercede: þingian *pres. subj. 3p.* 45, 57; þingigende *pres. p.* 1.
þis *pron.* this: þisses *ngs.* X54.
þoligan *w.2* lose: þolige *pres. subj. 3s.* X66.
þone *see* se.
þonne (1) *adv.* then 5, 13, 45, *etc.*; (2) *conj.* when 33, 42, 57, *etc.*; (3) *conj.* than 37.
þrēo *num.* three: -ra *g.* 3; þrywa three times 37, þriwa X54.
þridda *adj.* third: -n *mds.* X54, *mas.* X56.
geþristlǣcan *w.1* dare, presume: geþristlǣce *pres. subj. 3s.* 39.
ðrȳfeald *adj.* threefold: -re *fds.* X68e, f.
þrywa *see* þrēo.
þurfan *irreg.* need: þurfe *pres. subj. 3s.* X68i.
þurh *prep. w. acc.* through X16, 29.

GLOSSARY

unbiscopod *adj.* unconfirmed 15.
uncræft *m.* evil practice: **-um** *dp.* X68e.
ungedafenlic *adj.* unfitting: *nns.* 27.
under *prep. w. dat.* under 33, 38.
underfōn 7 receive: **underfō** *pres. subj. 3s.* 10.
unfæstende *adj.* without fasting 36.
unnit(t) *adj.* useless: *nas.* 26, *as noun* 26, 28, 68.
unriht *n.* (wrong): **mid unrihte** *ds. adv.* wrongly 14.
unwita *m.* fool: **-n** *as.* 4.
ūre see **wē**.

wā woe 39.
wanigan *w.2* lessen: **wanige** *pres. subj. 3s.* X68b.
warigan *w.2* be careful: **warige** *pres. subj. 3s.* 38.
warnigan *w.2* be careful: **warnige** *pres. subj. 3s.* X38.
wǣd *f.* garment: **-e** *ds.* 46; **-a** *gp.* X20.
(ge)wǣni(g)an *w.2* accustom (to): **wǣnige** *pres. subj. 3s.* 17; **gewǣnian** *pres. subj. 3p.* 55.
gewǣpned *adj.* armed X46.
wǣre, wǣs see **bēon**.
wǣter *n.* water 39; *as.* 43.
wē *pron.* we 1, 2, 3, *etc.*; **ūre** *g.* 47.
wealdan 7 control 26.
wel *adv.* well, wholly, truly 22, 29, 52, *etc.*
wēofod *n.* altar: **-e** *ds.* 31, 38, 44, *etc.*
wēofodsteall *m.* sanctuary: **-e** *ds.* X46.
wēofodþēn *m.* priest X68b, d; *as.* X68h.
wēohsteall *m.* sanctuary: **-e** *ds.* 46.
(ge)weorðan 3 (1) be, remain: **wurðe** *pres. subj. 3s.* 15; (2) happen: **gewurðe** *pres. subj.* 40.
weorðfull *adj.* honourable 59.
wer *m.* man 25; **-es** *gs.* X68d.
wīf *n.* wife: *as.* 25.
wīfman *m.* woman 44; **-na** *gp.* 61.
gewiglung *f.* spell: **-um** *dp.* 16.
willan *irreg.* wish: **wille** *pres. subj. 3s.* 22, 32, 47; **nele** *neg. pres. subj. 3s.* 22.
wilweorþung *f.* worship of (or at) wells: **-a** *ap.* 16.
wīn *n.* wine 39.
wīs *adj.* wise 59.
wīse *f.* manner, way: **wīsan** *as.* 48, 59, 69.
wīslīce *adv.* wisely 68.
gewita *m.* accessory 62.
witan *irreg.* know: **wite** *pres. subj. 3s.* 6, 29, 70.
gewitnes *f.* testimony: **-se** *ds.* 62.
wið *prep. w. dat.* with 38; *w. acc.* against 58, 60, 64.
world *f.* world: **-e** *ds.* 1.
worldafol *n.* worldly power: **-e** *ds.* 6.
worldhlāford *m.* secular master: **-um** *dp.* 1.
worldman *m.* layman: **-na** *gp.* 7.
woruldwīg *n.* earthly war: **-e** *ds.* X68b.
(ge)wurðe see **(ge)weorðan**.
wurðigan *w.2* honour: **wurðige** *pres. subj. 3s.* 2; **gewurðad** *pret. p.* 49.
wurðlīce *adv.* honourably, properly 33, 42.
wurðscipes see **wyrðscipe**.
wyrðe *adj. w. gen.* worthy of 22, 29.
wyrðscipe *m.* honour X68b; **wurðscipes** *gs.* X68d.

yfele *adv.* badly 6.
yldrum see **eald**.